Yami

the autobiography of Yami Lester

To my mother, Upitja, and to Lucy Lester.

First published in 1993 by
IAD Press
PO Box 2531
Alice Springs
NT 0871
Australia

© Yami Lester 1993

Reprinted 1995

Second edition published in 2000 by **jukurrpa books**,
an imprint of IAD Press.

Lester, Yami.
  Yami : the autobiography of Yami Lester.

  New ed.
  ISBN: 1 86465 025 7

  1. Lester, Yami. 2. Political activists - Australia - Biography.
  3. Aborigines, Australian - Australia, Central - Handicapped -
  Biography. 4. Aborigines, Australian - Australia, Central - Biography.
  5. Yankunytjatjara (Australian people) - Biography. I. Institute for
  Aboriginal Development (Alice Springs, N.T.). II. Title.

  305.89915

This book is copyright. Apart from any fair dealing for the purposes
of private study, research, criticism or review, as permitted under the
Copyright Act, no part may be reproduced by any process without
written permission. Please forward all inquiries to the Publisher at the
address below.

Maps by Brenda Thornley
Cover photograph by Mike Gillam
Films by Colorwize Studio. Printed by Hyde Park Press

Acknowledgements

The author and publisher wish to thank the following people for their time and effort in making this project possible: Donna Ah Chee, Angela Brennan, Andrew Collett, Cliff Goddard, John Henderson, Jenny Ince, Pamela Lyon, Maureen Tehan and Elizabeth Wood Ellem.

Our thanks also go to the many people who furnished us with or helped us in our search for photographs: the Lester family, Ray Beale, Bryan Charlton, Pauline Dunn, Bruce Evans, Doug Ewan, Eric Finck, Mertie Lander, Bill Lennon, Hazel and Brian Norris, Ron and Biddy Norris, Robin Percy, Charles Perkins, Tony Starkey, Dora Thompson, the staff of the State Reference Library of South Australia and the Australian Institute of Aboriginal and Torres Strait Islander Studies.

Daniel Vachon's work in transcribing and arranging the many hours of conversations which formed the basis of this book deserves special thanks. This story could not have been told in this way without Dan's creative and diligent involvement.

 This project was assisted by the Australia Council, the Federal Government's arts funding and advisory body.

The story of Yami's life reveals a man of courage and determination. This is an inspirational book.
Sally Morgan

Yami Lester is a strong and courageous Anangu man of Central Australia, a man of strength, experience and wisdom, a man who has overcome colonial adversity. His story is an inspiration to us all.
Mandawuy Yunupingu

Yami is riveting. From his early memories as a tribal boy, to the obviously pleasurable days of his youth as a stockman, to the harrowing narrative of the way he lost his sight, first in one eye, then, with surgical intervention, in the other, Yami shares with readers his joys and disappointments, as well as his boundless optimism and cheer.
Sydney Morning Herald

The story of Lester's time as a stockman and an activist for those blinded by the Maralinga nuclear tests deserves to be on the reading lists for students of Australian Studies. The deprivation of Lester's sight has been no impediment to his informal education which has taught him, among other things, to tell a story with ease and clarity.
The Sunday Age

The life of Yami Lester is one of understated courage and humility, told with gentle humour and sadness in the face of what most of us would consider astonishing adversity.
Habitat

Yami Lester's book has *kurun*, or 'spirit'. It grips the reader from the opening lines. The spirit of this book is more like that of Yami's dreaming name – *ngintaka*, the perentie (Australia's largest lizard): resourceful, tough, not scared to take on a big mob, whether they be opponents of land rights or politicians avoiding the consequences of Maralinga. It is a strong, exciting, often intense story.
The Advertiser

Yami is not the story of a man's rise to fame – it is the story of a human being who has met the challenges that life has presented him to the best of his ability, calling on his own inner resourses, sense of humour, and the encouragement and experience of his friends and acquaintances.
Centralian Advocate

Yami is a must for anyone interested in recent Australian history and is very entertaining.
Caroline Jones, The Search For Meaning

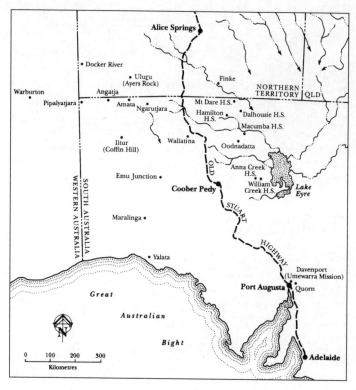

Central Australia, showing the area covered in Yami's story.

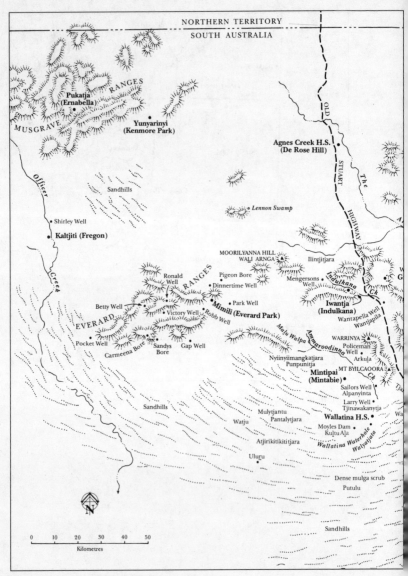

The far north of South Australia, showing the main creeks, waterholes, homesteads and communities around Wallatina.

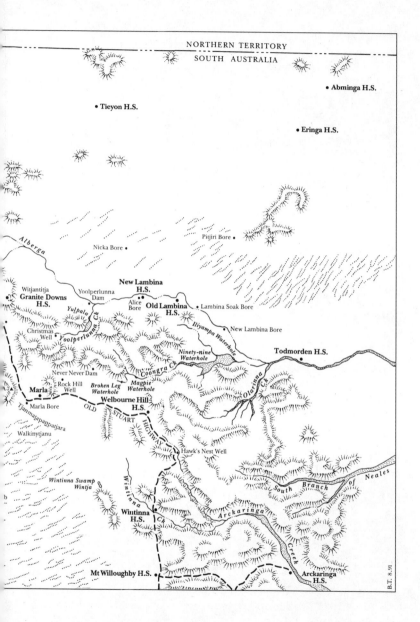

PROLOGUE

When I was a young boy living in the desert, the ground shook and a black mist came up from the south and covered our camp. The older people said they'd never seen anything like it before, and in the months that followed many people were sick and many died. I don't like to think about it now, but one of those people was my uncle, and he was very sick before he died.

People had sore eyes too. I was one of those people, and later on I lost my sight and my life was changed for ever. If I had my eyes, I would probably still be a stockman. Because I haven't, I became a stirrer.

I'm living in two worlds now: the world of the *wapar*, what you might call dreaming; and the world of the white people. Mine is just one of the stories of the Anangu, Aboriginal people of Central Australia. There are many other Anangu who have not had the opportunity to tell their stories.

But this is my story, and this is how it happened.

The Yankunytjatjara and Pitjantjatjara words used in this book are translated in notes at the end of each chapter.

1

Early Days

One of my earliest memories is of a trip we once made through the bush. We were living at Wintinna Station, north of Coober Pedy, where my mother, Pingkai, and my stepfather Kanytji worked. We set off to go to Arckaringa, another station south-east of Wintinna. No camels, walking. We had one big swag for the whole family, billycans and a digging stick. The men had spears and woomeras, and we had our two hunting dogs, Rover and Tingka.

We stopped at Mt Willoughby Station, where some of us kids went to the rubbish dump, looking for food. The Aboriginal women working at the homestead sang out, "*Awai!* Your father's going to hunt you away from there." That was my white father, Dick Lander, the manager of Mt Willoughby Station. "You gotta come this way," the women said, "and we'll give you some food." So we left the rubbish dump, but we didn't go to the house, we walked to the creek close by and waited until they brought out some food that my father gave to them: eggs and cake and different food.

That was as close as I got to my white father. I would like to have known him. But we couldn't have talked because I didn't have any English. I just had my own language, Yankunytjatjara. It would have been something that, to have talked with him. Anyway we did share something: he didn't want me to go to the rubbish dump!

My stepfather, Tjilpi Kanytji, got a job at Arckaringa, working as a shepherd for Colin Kennedy, who owned a mixed station – some cattle and some sheep. We lived out in a sheep camp, near a waterhole. He would yard the wethers up at night, and let them out next morning, shepherding them on foot, making sure they had enough feed. By and by, Kennedy would

3

come along in the truck with rations. I thought it was great: I liked the lollies. Mrs Kennedy made each of us kids a beautiful red dress with flowers and green leaves. Deadly. I think she thought I should be a girl. The older boys gave me a hard time. "Hey, what are you, a girl?" "Yeah," I said. "Stay away from me." I was quite happy: I had this beautiful dress on.

Shearing time, and Tjilpi Kanytji and Tjilpi Paddy Uluṟu used to draft all the sheep into the yard for the shearers. There was an engine going all day, with arms for the shears, and one bloke would chuck the wool in a big bag. After a while they'd chuck us kids in too and we'd jump up and down to press the wool in the bag for a tight fit. That was our job. After they'd shorn all the sheep, they'd load the bales of wool on a big truck for the railhead at Oodnadatta.

After the shearing we got a ride in the truck to Mt Willoughby, and from there we walked back to Wintinna. Tjilpi Kanytji got a job again with the station owner, Mr Giles, and my mother worked at the homestead. Our camp was a fair way out from the station, but us kids would hang around there. Sometimes we'd be a bit silly and they'd hunt us away. We used to shoot birds with shanghais and sometimes we might aim towards the house. There was five of us kids: Harry, Ginger, Uncle Bill Cullinan, me and my little brother. I don't feel right talking about my brother; I don't even want to say his name. He died when he was just a young man. I only have one brother left now, Shannon.

Up the creek from Wintinna Station there used to be a well, I forget the name. One time Phil Giles asked Stanley Lennon and Kanytji to shoot some brumbies out there. There was the biggest mob of wild horses. They'd shoot them when they came in for water. Then they cut off the horse's mane and the tail, and put them in a bag. That was their job. And I used to go too. As a little boy I used to stand with them, hiding with them in the pump-engine shed. The wild horses would come in, it was the biggest mob to me. They'd be standing and looking over to the stockyard and before they came into the yard to have a drink, Tjilpi Kanytji and Stanley just dropped them there with a big heavy gun, I think they called it a 303. They had about four guns, maybe more, and a lot of bullets.

One morning, I remember, they had two camels at the well. They decided to pick up the dead horses, pull them with the camels then take them away and burn them. So they put harnesses on the two camels and a long chain to tie to the dead horses. They tied this chain to one big old horse, dead about three or four days so there was plenty of juice and gravy. But they stopped the camels, and one of them said: "Wait on. Yami, you hold the camel, you know, just stand in front." Then they ran around the back of the horse to pick up its dead foal to put it on top of the carcass. While they were doing that one camel just looked at them out the corner of his eye, and then they both walked forward. They just pushed me over, I let go of the lead I was supposed to be holding, hung onto the chain, trying to get out, when the horse just came over me. I only had my head out and all my body got the gravy of that horse. It didn't hurt me but my pride was hurt and I was crying. I'd just gone out there after having a bath in a forty-four-gallon drum, nice clean shorts and shirt, and he just rubbished me again. And Stanley and Kanytji were still working away. "You all right? *Palya*?" I got all the gravy, beautiful, and I just smelt terrible. I walked back to the camp, crying all the way. Then my mother took the clothes and washed me again. Lucky there was other clothes for me.

Then one day Tjilpi Kanytji had a big argument with Phil Giles. It was about us kids. We'd been throwing rocks at birds hanging around the water tank, and somehow a rock got in the tank and blocked the outlet. It was a stupid thing to fall out over, but Phil and Kanytji had a real bust up – punches were thrown – and Kanytji walked off the job.

We set off at night and started walking hard, my little brother and me and my parents – no tucker, just the swag and a billy. Tjilpi Kanytji was frightened, he thought Phil Giles might come after him because he pulled out of the job. By the next morning we were out in the bush somewhere, a rocky place on top of a hill with witchetty-grub bushes growing around. It wasn't a good place – too many rocks and not enough shade.

5

There was a little water left in the billycan. My mother put special grass in the water, *wanguṉu*, I think. When you drink, you just sip a little through the grass, so you make that water last all day and maybe all night.

It took us two days through the bush, no meat and not much water, but at last we made it to Kanytji's brother's camp. Kanytji's brother worked this sheep camp for Phil Giles, and Phil had been around asking after us, so we hung low for a while. A few days later, when Mr Giles came round with the rations, he saw Tjilpi Kanytji. I was pretty scared at first, but they made up, and Phil asked Kanytji to come back to work for him. So we got in the truck and went back to Wintinna Station.

Another time, my parents decided to go to a place called Wallatina. There was a group of us travelling. We carried a little bit of tea and sugar, but picked up most of our food as we went along. We reached a stony place along the creek where there was a well. From here we went west, cross-country to that big swamp, Wintjanya. After a few days, though, I thought we were going to die. Our water was finished. One person had half a billy of water but because it was getting heavy, they'd left it along our track. That night we camped – no water – and next morning we started off again. It was too hot and I was tired. We dug a hole in the ground in the shade and lay down in it. Ready to finish I suppose.

Kanytji told us not to move while he went off with a billy-can; he knew a rockhole that sometimes had water. That evening he came back with a little water in the billycan that he'd got from that rockhole. I was really thirsty but he put some on his hand and just wet my lips. "Just a little bit, not too much," he said, "or you'll get sick, you'll vomit up." Then we boiled the billy and drank some tea and felt better.

That night we had to walk in the dark, heading for that rock-hole. We stopped there and camped for two nights while we recovered. Then we filled the billycans and headed for that creek called Walkinytjanu. We had to reach that one, and I think it took us a good bit of twenty-four hours to get there. Big soak-age, and when we got there we sat down to rest another day.

6

The next afternoon we arrived at that *ngintaka ngura* – that old perentie lizard's place, Wallatina.

Awai! – "Hey there!"
tjilpi – old man, elder (term of respect)
palya – OK
wangunu – naked woollybutt grass
ngintaka ngura – perentie lizard's place or camp

Ngintaka

This is *Ngintaka*, the perentie lizard. Once in the *wapar* he was *anangu*, a person, and he came a long way from the west.

Just south of Wallatina Homestead is a little creek called Walyatjata. There's a *nyintjiri* community at Walyatjata Water-hole, and that *ngintaka* sat down there with them. The *nyintjiri* people had a beautiful *tjiwa* at Walyatjata, a beautiful grinding stone.

On the fourth day, *ngintaka* says, "Hey, why don't we all go hunting for meat?" So everybody, men and women, left the community, and they go off to Tjinawakanytja (Larry Well they call it now). When he's there *ngintaka* says he staked his foot on a stick. That's why it's called *tjina wakanytja*. And everybody, all the *nyintjiri* said: "Oh *tjamu*, grandfather, you poor thing. Your foot's hurt." They tied his foot up with hair string and told him, "*Tjamu*, you wait here and we'll go for meat." So they went around to that Walkinytjanu Creek, following it up, hunting.

As soon as they've gone from his sight, *ngintaka* runs back to Wallatina Waterhole and grabs the *tjiwa*, that beautiful grinding stone. He lets out a lot of his *kurun* then, to cover up his tracks. He multiplies them, leaving spirit footprints all around. Then he heads out west with the *tjiwa*.

Malu, the red kangaroo, comes through then, nearby Walyatjata with *kanyala*, that euro. Two men on a long journey with their uncle, *tjurki*, the nightjar, see the tracks. "Oh, old *ngintaka*'s been around here, hum?" They pick up his track, where he goes back to Walyatjata, the old bastard! And they see all the people, the *nyintjiri* people at Wallatina Waterhole. They go north then, to Ikaltji and Malu Walpa, and north again from there.

Ngintaka was taking his time, he wasn't in a hurry. He stops at every place, gave it a name, sits down and makes *inma* about that place. No worries. He never thought about any trouble.

He goes to Waḻi Arnga, Moorilyanna Hill. So people from that country got that story, that's their line. He goes to a place near Mimili, that's Bruce Woodford's *ngura* – he's a relative of mine. And then he travelled to Shirleys Well, near Officer Creek, and so the Shirleys Well people have the *ngiṉṯaka wapar*.

Further west, at Ngarutjara (Mt Woodroffe), *ngiṉṯaka* sat down for a long time. He saw people a long way off and he made *inma*. He seen *mala* people, and that dangerous snake at Uluṟu, and he saw that dingo spirit-monster catch the hare-wallabies on top of the Rock. (He's still there at Mt Woodroffe, chest out, standing up and having a good look.)

And he made rain, lot of rain. He made all the *inma* about rain. He sang and the black clouds came over him. And as he went along making rain, travelling with a song, he made food: *parka-parka* and *ngantja, kaḻtu-kaḻtu, wakati, kunakanti*. The whole lot. He made food for people that *ngiṉṯaka*, that rogue.

When the *nyinṯjiri* mob got back from hunting, they followed the *ngiṉṯaka* tracks to Wallatina Waterhole. And there's one little boy left behind at the camp. He saw *ngiṉṯaka* come back and take the *tjiwa*. So all the *nyinṯjiri* start following the tracks, and the little boy says: "Hey, this is it. This is the right track." The men reckon: "Get lost kid. Piss off." But the boy says: "But that's not it, it's this one. I know him, we were friends. He's got the *tjiwa* and gone. This is his track. All those are just spirit footprints he made."

They didn't take any notice of the boy. Anyway, by and by, one of them does. Then they start following his track, and they followed it and followed it and followed it. But they had to stop all along the way because it kept raining. Then they caught up with *ngiṉṯaka*. "Hey, where's that *tjiwa*? Come on." "What *tjiwa*?" *ngiṉṯaka* says. "Oh, not me. I left it behind." So they touched him all over. Turned him over on his back, legs up in the air, and started feeling around his belly. But nothing. "True, there's nothing. I don't know what he's done with it." "Behind," he says, "I left it behind." And they ran all the way back to Wallatina Waterhole. They're a stupid mob. It was behind all

9

right. He had that *tjiwa* right on the end of his tail!

And *ngintaka* started travelling west again. He went to Angatja, right up to Walytjatjata, near the Western Australian border, and past Walytjatjata. Then his auntie saw him, she could see the rain clouds getting closer and closer. "One more night. Just one more night," she says, "and my nephew will be here." So he was just one night away. He made camp and went for a piss. Left the *tjiwa* behind.

Then the *nyintjiri* mob arrived. They saw it. "Hey, that *tjiwa*'s been there all the time. He had it all the time, the bastard!" So, they started stomping on it with their feet, whoomp whoomp, breaking it.

Ngintaka heard the noise, so he raced back to his *tjiwa* camp. "*Ngangkarku!* Heck! Oh, no!" The *nyintjiri* saw him and they threw their spears at him, but he beat the whole lot. But this one bloke, left-handed fella, he got him then. And you can see the place there, you can see which one throws the last spear and hits him. They cut him up, opened him up, and he's there now, one big smooth rock, like a big stone pipe. Place called Arannga. That's where he finished up.

And his auntie saw the rain clouds breaking up then; she knew that her nephew was not going to make it. That was it.

* * *

I'm a *ngintaka*. And I suppose I'm a *nyintjiri* too. Poor things. Poor, crummy little *nyintjiri*.

I was born at Walyatjata, near the waterhole there, Wallatina Waterhole. They told me, maybe if I want to, I might be *malu*, that kangaroo, because it's close by. But the more they thought about it, they said, that *ngintaka* was mine. Me. It was like that.

So I'm a *ngintaka*, from where I was born. Everyone has one of those *wapar*. My stepfather, Kanytji, is *kanytjil*; Kanytji is one of the bosses for that *tjalku*. My mother, Pingkai, is different again.

They told me that *ngintaka* story when I was a little bit older.

They said, "This is *ngintaka* dreaming." Not dreaming, but *ngintaka wapar*. They used the word *wapar*, Pitjantjatjara use *tjukurpa*. Some people say dreaming. But it's not a dream. It's real to me and it means something. *"Nyuntumpa ngura,"* they told me, "Your place." Walyatjata and Tjinawakanytjanya, my country.

And they told me about *malu* and *kanyala* and their uncle the nightjar; about their track; which way they come. Because I was only *tjitji*, a kid, they just told me what they do, where they go: Ulurunya, Watjunya, Mulytjantunya, Pantalytjaranya, all those places nearby Walyatjata. *Malu* gives those names, and other places, *ngintaka* names them. They said it was important, very important *wapar*.

They told me about *malu* and the honey ants, and about *malu* making the language for us. How that *malu* would try out the food that was already there. "Ah, no," he'd say. "This is for animals to eat." Other food, he'd say, "Ah, now this is for people." He would try to taste that *untanu-untanu*. "No, nothing this one, rubbish, don't worry about it." It's just to look at. And there's one like a *tawal-tawal*. It's a high prickly bush with berries like a *tawal-tawal*. Kids can easily make a mistake. Adults teach you when *malu* ate that, he'd say, "No, this is only for kangaroos." But that *tawal-tawal*: "Great. Now this is for boys and girls."

That's how they'd tell the story. They'd tell you it's real, they believed it. I don't know if Pingkai and Kanytji were Christians. I don't know what they knew when I was a kid. They never talked to me about it, they just talked about the country. And I believed what they said. You couldn't doubt, it was just something real. The country wasn't just hills or creeks or trees. And I didn't feel like it was fairy tales they told me. It was real, our *kuuti*, the force that gives us life. Somebody created it, and whoever created it did it for us, so we could live and hunt and have a good time. That's how we come to be here because that *malu* and *ngintaka* created this image for us to live and breathe: the plants, the language, the people. And to have rain, wind and rain. At Mt Woodroffe *ngintaka* made a song about wind, so the Ones Who Know can sing it today. If somebody gets wild, he can sing it and make a strong wind.

The spirits of that *ngintaka* and the *nyintjiri* live in the hills around Wallatina. The hills belong to them, even the stones lying on the ground. When I was a kid going around the country I might see a nice-looking stone and like to pick it up. But the Ones Who Know would tell us very, very seriously that anything like that, perhaps a *kanti*, or a piece of red ochre, it still belongs to them. OK, it was *wapar*, but they are living there. Only we can't see them with our naked eyes. Only *ngangkari* can see them walking around, looking at you, smiling at you and all that. "They're there all the time," our elders would say. "You can't see them, but they're there. Watching you. You can't just take nice stones without asking." Then they'd say, "This is the way you do it. You must talk to them properly. Like this: 'Ah, sorry, but ah… the other day I dropped a *kanti* somewhere around here. And ah… I think it's this one! Yeah, this is it. I must've left it near this windbreak.'" Like that. And while you're going around talking to them you might be filling your bag up.

Then there's *ampaka*. I think the *nyintjiri* mob say *ampaka*. It's a Yankunytjatjara word. I don't know what it means, but *ampaka* is *ampaka*. They're out there: women, *tjitji* and men. *Tjitji* girl, *tjitji* boy, all that. Even *papa ampaka* – they got dogs too. So they'd teach us kids about those *ampaka*. Anywhere you go – Wintinna, Welbourne Hill, out from Wallatina – if you want to take something from the ground, you must ask the *ampaka* in the proper way. Because those *ampaka* are all over this land, all the way to Oodnadatta.

So those *ampaka* are watching you, and they're happy you're asking before taking anything. It's all right. But we were told if you don't ask, if you just go picking things up, then something'll happen to you. You'll get sick or something. They'll put a whole lot of stones in your body and *ngangkari* will have to work on you, take those stones out. They always blame that *ngintaka*. He's there and he'll do something because you've been silly – taking things without asking. He can do that.

These days you might be driving a car and get a flat tyre, then another one. On and on like that. Or there's something

12

wrong with your car, you might blow a motor. When that happens some people say, "Oh yeah, well that's *ngintaka* for you. Playing up on you because you didn't do the right thing." And at Angatja, west of Amata, when Charlie Ilyitjari takes tourists around, he tells them about that. Same *ngintaka* went through his wife's place. If they don't do what he says at the caves there, if they just go in anyway, something will happen to them. They have got to be careful, do the right thing.

So what I do when I go to that *ngintaka* waterhole, where he came and took that *tjiwa*, I have got to throw a stone into the creekbed and say, "Oh, I've just come for nothing, just to say 'good day'. *Wai*, you all right?" And it's all right then. They're good to you. They look after you.

It's the kind of thing we learned when we were kids. It was really serious. It was important for us to learn it. So we did, and learned it well.

I was proud I was part of the *ngintaka* family. People recognise that we are different from *malu* and all the others. That was part of it. People can look at you and say, "Oh, he's different." Different face or different features. "He's a *ngintaka*."

I used to like eating *ngintaka* meat once. But every time I ate it I couldn't sleep. It just felt like *ngintaka* was walking in my guts all night. It used to be like that for a long time, so I asked *tjilpi tjuta*, the Ones Who Know: "Why is it every time I eat *ngintaka*, it does that to me? Why is it?" And they said: "Well, *ngintaka* is you, you know, that's your *wapar*. You're a *ngintaka wapar*. You shouldn't eat it, just leave it alone. Every time you eat that, he'll do that to you." So I don't eat it now. That's the spirit. *Ngintaka* is me and I shouldn't eat myself.

But I can eat goanna and kangaroo. Sometimes we might see a big old kangaroo close to the camp. Just sitting there. Somebody might say: "Hey, there's a kangaroo. Let's shoot it." Then I say: "Nah, leave him. He's too close to the camp. That could be our *tjamu*." So they'll leave him. Go further out and get a kangaroo. "Now this is real meat," they'll say. "I think that other one was that old fella, you know?" Same for *ngintaka* near your camp. Or an eagle might come close. "Hey, that might be our

13

son. Leave it alone."

They stick in my mind, those stories. Now when I travel and meet up with those people, they say to me: "You're from Walyatjata? Come on, we'll show you where that *ngintaka* took the *tjiwa* from your country." They say they will show me that place, Arannga, where *ngintaka* finished up, but I haven't seen it yet. "There's the *tjiwa*," they'd say. "The one *ngintaka* pinched from Yami's place. What a rotten old bloke that *ngintaka* is."

If he had not taken the *tjiwa*, Walyatjata would have been called Tjiwa Piti. Everybody would go there and carry out the ceremony to get a *tjiwa*. All the grinding stones would have been there. But because he ended up at the other end, nearly to the Western Australian border, I think that's how Tjiwa Piti came to be there.

And *ngintaka*'s still taking that *tjiwa* on the end of his tail, they say. And *ngintaka* is still singing.

ngintaka – perentie lizard

anangu – person

Anangu – Aboriginal person, usually, but not always, from the Western Desert region

tjiwa – grinding stone

tjamu – grandfather

wapar – 'dreaming', law

nyintjiri – small, inedible lizard

tjina wakanytja – staked foot

kurun – spirit

ngura – place

mala – rufous hare-wallaby

ngantja – mistletoe

wakati – pig weed

inma – traditional song

ngintaka wapar – perentie lizard dreaming

parka-parka – mistletoe

kaltu-kaltu – bush millet

kunakanti – grass seed

ngangkarku – exclamation, oh heck

kanytjil – pig-footed bandicoot

tjalku – bilby

malu – red kangaroo

tjitji – child, children

tawal-tawal – wild gooseberry

kanti – a sharp stone for a blade

kanyala – euro

untanu–untanu – flowers of mulga bush

ngangkari – healer, traditional doctor

papa – dog

Wai? – "What's up?"

ampaka – ethereal gnome-like creatures

14

Wallatina Days

I remember Wallatina as my place. When I saw the camp there, there was the biggest mob of people. Well, to me it looked like a lot of people. You could say forty or fifty. And the kids! I knew some of the people in the camp. They used to be at Wintinna and now they were all back at Wallatina. They used to come and go all the time. Of course, Kanytji and my mother knew everybody. They'd say to me, "Oh, that man's your *mama*. He's my elder brother, so he's your *mama*." Or my mother might say, "Now that woman's my *untal*, so she's your *kangkaru*."

And then she'd say: "Now those two men, they're my *katja* and they're your elder brothers. So you call them *kuta*." Like that. Because I was a whitefella's son, my half-brother and I called some of our relatives differently. They'd say: "When you call your relations, you're not for Kanytji. You're for Pingkai, your mother." My half-brother calls them from both sides. He might take Tjilpi Kanytji's line or our mother's line. One of my *kami*, my half-brother calls *kangkaru*. I'd learn from them like that.

Our grandfather, Dick Wallatina, was there. He was a proper Yankunytjatjara and Matutjara, my grandfather. Poor thing. He was a number-one man for places around my country: Pantalytjara, Multjantu, and Alpanyinta. His wife was there, too, my grandmother and Kukika's mother. Another old fella, Witapitjanu, was also at Wallatina. He was an important man, a *ngangkari*; he had lots of authority in the community and we had lots of respect for him. He used to make songs. Everybody in the camp would dance to them at night.

And there was Kelly. Kelly was a bit older, but we were good mates. He was my track mate. And Uncle Harry Wallatina, a beautiful man. He was *nyiinka* then, and he had his own camp away from the rest. My uncle, a *nyiinka*! Me and Kelly used to go and camp with him, and he'd look after us. He was good to us and we were good to him. Sometimes my mother and father would go away, maybe to see people at other stations – Mimili or Granite Downs – and I'd be staying back at Wallatina with my uncle.

When we first arrived at Wallatina we lived just to the south of Cullinans' place, out in the open, near a small sandhill. But we'd move the camp around. Once we lived right near the Cullinans'. At another time we were to the east, and once just to the north. We never had a camp on the south, it was too open and windy.

Kanytji worked for the Cullinans. Mr and Mrs Cullinan didn't have much. They didn't have sheep, just cattle and goats. They lived in sort of a house made from sheet-of-iron, near the stockyard and well. They had a little store, and Tommy Cullinan would look after the government rations: flour, tea, sugar, black treacle. The rations came in on the mail truck from Oodnadatta.

People in the camp got rations once a week all the time we were there. But we used to run out maybe on the third or fourth day. We didn't worry about it. We just lived from the bush then.

Sometimes my mother would help at the house, but Mrs Cullinan already had *tjamu* Dick's two daughters, Kanginy and Kukika, and my mother's sister, Eileen Brown, working there. And my *ngunytju* (you might say younger mother) was there too. She's Ronnie Russell's missus now. She used to look after the nanny-goats.

Tommy Cullinan was a good old fella. He used to drop a killer for us. Other times, when him and his wife might be away, people used to break into the store. They would just take out a few nails and get flour, tea, sugar and treacle. It was only a tin shed, but it was his main store and he kept his things there. As soon as the Cullinans came home, they'd tell them they had broken in. Tommy Cullinan would say: "Oh, *palya*. No worries." That's why I say he was a lovely man, Tjilpi Cullinan. I liked him.

16

The Cullinans didn't have many cattle. They used to be mainly around Sailors Well and Larry Well (Tjinawakanytja, where that *ngintaka* staked his foot) and Wallatina Waterhole. Sometimes, after the rain, his cattle used to go where Moyles Dam is now, Kultu Alanya. Tjilpi Cullinan would chase the cattle in his old truck: "Better take 'em back, the bastards. They've come too far out."

The men would do cattle work for him. And they would build stockyards, like the one at Larry Well. Kanytji and Uncle Harry dug wells all over the place. Tjilpi Cullinan would give them pay in the end. One time I saw him counting out and paying those two men the biggest mob of money: notes and shillings. Lotta green notes.

I never heard Kanytji complain about the cattle or about Tommy Cullinan, but I remember my mother one time complaining to Kanytji about the pay and he said: "No, it's good enough. I'm getting tucker to feed you and the kids, that's good enough. I don't have to ask the boss for pay. What's it got to do with pay anyway?" So they're just having a family discussion. I don't think they saw Tommy Cullinan as trespassing on the country. Well, they might have talked about it, but they didn't say anything to me. When older people sat down and talked, the kids went and played.

Our home in Wallatina was a pretty happy place. We had plenty to eat. We lived around there for a long time. Not in houses: everybody had *kanku*, what the Pitjantjatjara call *wiltja*, a sort of a bush house made of sticks and spinifex and sometimes canvas. Dry and warm, they were. Except one time there was a big rain and water just went through all of them. The ground around the homestead was no good when there was a big rain. A sheet of water just lay on the top of the ground. Everything was wet: blankets, flour, tea, sugar. Finished. One *kanku* had been next to the little creek, and it was just gone. *Tjamu* Dick and Kanytji and a couple of other fellas – I reckon there were only six men in the camp – made a shelter out of a big mulga tree and lit a big fire out in the thunder and lightning and rain.

17

We didn't spend much time in the camp, there was too much to do. There were a lot of boys to play with, and we'd go out to the small hill nearby and make out we were hunting *kanyaḻa*. But they were all just *tjati*. And we'd spear them with our little spears and then hit them with our *tjuṯiny*. "*Palatai!* Over there! *Kanyaḻa! Kanyaḻa!*" Make out, you know.

When I wasn't with kids my age, I'd sit down with those *nyiiṉka*, who'd be in their own camp away from the others. They're not allowed to see the women. Uncle Harry was a wild one, I could never find his camp. I would go, "*Ai!*", and because he can't sing out, he used to hit the ground with his *tjuṯiny*. Kelly was there too, later on, when he was *nyiiṉka*. I used to go take food to him: tea, damper, meat. The *nyiiṉka* would just go hunting by themselves. They wouldn't keep asking for food, like today.

I remember that one time the biggest mob of *nyiiṉka* came to Wallatina from Mimili: Teddy Edwards, Johnny Wangin, and a lot of others. They had a big *nyiiṉka* camp, and I used to take tea and damper for them. All the mothers and other relations used to ask me to go, because the other kids just wanted to play. They would say: "Yaminyampa! Oh, there you are. Wait a minute, here, take this meat to your older brother. They tell us he's out there someplace." All right, then. I stopped the game I'd been playing, and take it out to them. I used to like to do that. Sometimes they'd give me dampers cooked in fat and they'd put a stick through maybe five or six of them. They made me hungry. So I'd take it over and I'd say to those *nyiiṉka*, "This is supposed to be for all of us they told me." They never said anything. Just told me to sit down and we'd have a feed. I was like that. I used to tell little lies when I was hungry.

There were activities in the camp for everybody – men and women and kids – like they have in the communities today. I've seen the adults go off for business too, but that's all I saw because I was *tjiṯji*, just a kid. They'd go out bush away from the camp, leaving us kids there.

When there was women's business, I'd be in charge of looking after the other kids. We'd come near to the Cullinans' tin

18

shed with our dinner bags and play in the mulga trees that used to be there. We played men-on-horses and things like that. Making out that we were like men on horses, but there were no horses, of course. There was an old racetrack there, where I used to sit down and look after the kids. Well, I was supposed to. But one day I didn't do a head count, and one bloke was missing. And that was Shannon, my little brother. I didn't know what to do, so we just sat down and had our dinner. We watched the sun starting to go down and thought about going to the camp. Or maybe we should wait for our mothers and aunties to come back, we thought. Turns out that Shannon followed them to the women's ceremony place, proudly going along with his dog on a chain. But they saved him and brought him back, crummy little kid.

Just about every evening in the main camp there'd be *inma*, singing and dancing Yankunytjatjara songs. It was a happy time. Tjilpi Cullinan was in his house, no worries, and we were over in the camp at *inma*. And Witapitjanu, he used to make Tjilpi Kanytji work all the time, dancing *inma*. During the day Kanytji'd work for Tommy Cullinan, and when he knocked off he'd come back to the camp, drink some tea, have a damper, then he'd be missing. Gone bush. Then Witapitjanu would come over before supper: "*Tjuu! Tjuu!* Hey let's go. *Walangkuya!* Hurry up!" So we all would go to that place where they sit down and sing *inma*. He'd tell us to hide our faces, so we couldn't see. Then, "*Pakara nyawa!* Come on, everybody! Get those blankets off your heads and have a look!" And there some people would be, standing there, just about to dance. Gee, they were good dancers, but the main one was Kanytji. That old Witapitjanu, he used to make him work hard.

When *inma* was finished, we ate supper, and they'd tell us bedtime stories. We lay in the swag and listened and mumbled: "Uh hum, yes, yes," nodding our heads until we fell asleep. *Tjitji* finished.

They've got a lot of stories, called *wapar*. One was about this *wati*, travelling by himself and carrying a *tjiwa*. He spears some meat, carries it off, cooks it and eats a piece. Then he starts off again, carrying the meat all cut up. He gets to a waterhole and looks around, thinking to himself: "Now where can I make a camp? Oh, well, here will do." Then he looks up. "Hey, *ngangkarpa*, heck! Clouds. Storm clouds coming up and what am I going to do? I've got no *kanku*, and it's going to rain." Then thunder, and it's raining. And then the *tjiwa* he's been carrying turns into a big cave. He sleeps in the cave that night, with his spears and meat and everything. Then he gets up in the morning, nice and dry, and the cave becomes a little *tjiwa* again. So off he goes, and every night that *tjiwa* turns into a nice, warm cave for him. Then maybe at his third or fourth camp he sees another *tjiwa*. So he throws away the first one and takes the new one he found. This one's bigger and it looks better. When night comes, he makes a camp. Storm clouds again and it starts to rain again. "No worries," he says, "I've got no *kanku*, but I've got this nice big *tjiwa*." Nothing happens. It is raining and raining and still he is waiting for that *tjiwa* to get up and make a cave. In the end, hailstones fall and kill him. Finished. It turns out that the first *tjiwa* he was carrying was his mother, and the second one he picked up was his *kungka umari*. Because a man and his mother-in-law can't sit close to each other, or talk to each other, she was too shy to make a cave for him. So the rain killed him. Finished. End of story. They told us kids stories like that.

During the day, if they didn't go out hunting, the men'd be sitting down making spears or boomerangs or wooden dishes, things like that. And they would show us how to make them. When they made boomerangs they used to cut trees already having a boomerang curve. Today they got a more technical way of doing it and a better style. They used to use them in *inma*, not for hunting or selling to tourists. Oh, but sometimes they might use them in a fight.

Just about every day the women would leave the camp and go for rabbits, *maku*, honey-ants, all that. Taking digging sticks and *wira* made out of wood or maybe an old car's mudguard, billycans, and us kids. Just walking. No camels or horses or motor car. Out in the bush, they would collect different kinds of grass seeds, like *wangunu*. They use to take that and make little cakes. They put honey-ants with it. Beautiful, beautiful. *Wangunu* and honey-ants. At Mimili they used to do that with *iḻi*. They used to dry *iḻi*, and eat them later. Another grass seed was *wakati*. I didn't like it very much. The seeds were black. *Kunakanti* was a grass of the same family. Another they collected was called *kaḻtu-kaḻtu*. You might call it native millet. *Kuṟara*, from that dead-finish bush, I used to eat it fresh. I'd go and just stand there and eat like a galah! The women used to get biggest mob, pod them, and put them in their *wira*. When they dried, they would grind them up on a *tjïwa*. We'd eat little dampers made from those seeds and that *kuṟara* all the time.

And then there was *tjuntala* and *waṭarka*. We got that too, just down from the camp. Us kids used to help them collect it; put it in *wira* for all the *kungka tjuṭa*. They'd say: "This is good food. He'll come good when we cook it later on. Come on, give us a hand." So we used to pick them. We used to play and pick it at the same time. And we were quicker than they were. Then they would take them back to the camp and cook them in the hot earth. And we'd eat it.

And there was another one, I forget the name, like a carrot. It grows in stony country. It was short and fat, and they used to dig them out. Gee, it was beautiful. And *urpa*, like a carrot again, but thinner. I didn't like it as much. They'd teach us about that one too. "This is *urpa*," they'd say. "It's a food called *urpa*. This is your grandmothers' and grandfathers' food. Real food to make you bigger." We used to dig *urpa* up for them, the biggest mob. They'd cook it in the hot earth mainly, not in the coals. Then they'd get it out quickly and give it to us. And we'd have a good old feed.

And they told us about bush medicines. There was that bush called *ipi ipi*. They'd put that in the fire and the smoke would make a sick person feel better. And another one, *aratja*, was a dark-green bush with a strong smell. The juice from the leaves was used for rubbing medicine if we got a cold. That's two I remember, but there were a lot more. And they even got that *maku* for medicine. OK, it's good to eat, but they'd also take a fresh one and use the insides to put on a sore. And I can remember them taking spider webs and wrapping them around cuts on our fingers.

And there's *walkal*. We can't touch that. It would kill people. They'd only use it if they want to poison emu. They'd get the leaves, then grind them to get the juice out, add water to it, then put it in a little rockhole. So the emu will drink the poison water, because they'd close up the main water with heavy timber. When the emu drank it his legs just went stiff, I think, and they could follow him then.

We had flour, tea and sugar, too. You know, rations. But we were eating *mai*, vegetable food we got from the bush. They'd make a damper with that and leave the flour in the bag for later on. Plenty time. I remember seeing *piti*, those big wooden dishes, on top of my mother's *kanku*, full of those seeds. It was the same at the place of my grandmother, Harry Wallatina's mother's place. They'd keep it, grind it up, cook it: "You want something to eat?" And we'd eat it. Our grandmothers' and grandfathers' food.

There was always tucker. No worries, we were never short. The women would teach us about the country and the food. *Maku* and *tawal-tawal* and *kampurara*. They were good. The Ones Who Know would say, "Now this one is different again. You call it *wiriny-wiriny*, bush tomato." It's really beautiful, that one. It has a lovely smell. We'd get greedy for that; we don't want to share it with anybody.

When I wasn't out with the kids and the women, I used to follow *tjamu* Dick, our grandfather: "Come on, grandson. It's all right, you can come." He was a good old fella, lovely man. He used to speak in a deep voice in Matutjara, an old language a bit like Yankunytjatjara. That Wallatina Waterhole is Yankunytjatjara and Matutjara. And they sing *ngintaka inma* in Matutjara. Dick would just have his spears. No dog. The best time for hunting was *piriyakutu*, when the hot north wind blew in the spring. He'd teach me: "Now what we're doing, grandson, is *wampatananyi, wampata ngali yananyi* [hunting alone, one man hunting]." I was there too, of course, but I was only *tjitji*, tagging along, supposed to keep out of the way.

22

Just to the east of the homestead, it was swamp country when it rained. Hard clay ground and lot of good mulga, good shade for *malu*. One day we went there and I think he saw one *malu*, but I couldn't see it. That *malu* had his face hidden by a tree-trunk. But my *tjamu*, he must've seen the tail and rear end. He whispered to me: "Grandson. Come over here and sit down. Just watch and don't move." He sneaks up, lifts one foot, and stops. Stands like that for a long time – well, it seemed like a long time to me – then, very slowly, he puts it down. Goes forward like that. Then I seen him aim with his spear, throw it and hit the *malu*. He called out, "Grandson!" And I started walking over with the other spears he'd left with me. I could see him hitting the *malu* with a stick. When I got to him, that *malu* was finished and our grandfather was really happy. He took out the *tjuni*, gave me the lower intestines to carry, and said: "Now you just carry this *tjuni*. When I give this *malu* to someone, I don't know who'll cook it, you gotta leave that with him. That *tjuni* is his. If you sit down quietly, he might give you part of it to eat. That's the way it is." Then he closed up the *malu* and carried him back to camp on his head. Poor thing. He's a lovely man.

When we got back to the camp, one of the men there said he'd be the cook, so we gave it to him. There was always somebody willing to cook then. Not like today. You might drive up in your Toyota and say, "Hey, there's *malu* here." And they'll just say: "Oh, right. Wait a minute, why don't you take it someplace else? I've got no firewood." Lazy buggers, always got excuses.

So the man took it from my grandfather, built a big fire, and threw the kangaroo in to burn off the fur. I knew you couldn't just cook *malu* any way, Kanytji'd taught me that. I remember him telling me: "Now, this is the way you do it. If you break the rules, there's one way left – death. You gotta do this properly. If you don't, they'll kill you. Or kill me."

So I watched him dislocate the two back legs, cut the tail off at just the right spot, and put it in the small trench he had dug, with the tail beside the body, and cover it up with ashes and sand. Then I went to have a sleep. When I got up and went over, they had taken it out and were cutting it up in the proper way. The upper part of the body was our grandfather's, because he was the hunter. He called me over: "Grandson, give me a hand." He was taking the liver and kidneys out and telling me: "This is the way you do it, like this. It's *wapar*, you know, no lie." Then he cut the rest of him down. The cook got the tail. And they shared the rest with other people in the camp.

So I was busy all the time. That was my school, my education. Going out and learning from different people. It always happened like that. And it was good.

* * *

I'll never forget a trip I took with Kanytji once, just him and me. He decided to go to a place called Malu Walpa inside Granite Downs boundary, looking for dingoes. At that time dingo scalps fetched one pound a head. We walked north towards a soakage called Mintipainya. Kanytji would tell me the places as we went along, teaching me the country, about the *waparitja*. We saw a wild cat on the way and he speared the cat, but it went into a hole. It still had a spear in its body, so I pulled it out. Tjilpi said, "Look out. It'll bite you, scratch you." So I killed it with a *tjutiny*. We got a couple of rabbits too.

Then we got to Mintipai. There was an old opal mine there that Tjilpi Tommy Cullinan and maybe a few others put in before. Wasn't much to worry about. Pick and shovel job. Nothing like the Mintabie Opal Field there today. Kanytji dug out the soakage, and built it up like a well, and we waited for the water to come up. Then we had a drink and enough to fill the billycan. We boiled up the tea and ate rabbit and pussy cat. Then we travelled on, carrying the water in the billycan. It was cool time, so it was quite pleasant to go on foot. We camped near a big hill and got the fire going. I think we just had a blanket each. He carried the blankets strapped on his back.

Next morning we went up and over the hill and came to another place. I think it was Punpunitjanya. Then we followed the creek up and we camped. We came to Nyiinyiimangkatjara then. I suppose you could translate that as "the place where the zebra finch had a mop of hair on his head". When I was a kid it appealed to me, that place. You can look away to the creek there and in the distance is a stand of nice cassia bushes, *punti tjaṯa*. And on the north side there's a little round hill. There're happy features about the place. I just liked it.

There weren't very many dingoes around, and so after a few days, Kanytji decides to go back to Mintabie. So we walk flat out, you know, not stopping and looking for food, just straight walking. Up and over a hill, then we turned left to get *urtjan*. Just one *urtjan* tree grows there; might still be there. Nearby is a bit of a cave and a different type of *mingkuḻ* inside. It's called *pitur* and it's like *mingkuḻ*, but more strong. I think we got three or four *urtjan*, then we come out the same way along sort of a valley where a creek goes up to that place. Really dangerous place. If *kuṯaṯji* or *warmaḻa* (revenge party, you might say) can get you in there, they'll take your life.

We got to Mintabie on dusk. He quickly threw the sand from that soakage he dug two, three days ago. We waited and got the water. The sun was down then, but it was still sort of light. On a sandhill, he said, "We'll make camp here in this mulga. I'll light the fire and you might get some wood." Nice sheltered mulga. So I walked a few feet away from the camp and saw the biggest mob of wood heaped up. So I gave him two logs and I got two logs for myself. "No worries," I told him. We had a drink of tea and went to sleep pretty early. It was wintertime. That night I dreamed this *mamu*, sort of a harmful spirit, got me. I jumped up and said, "*Paiya!*" Kanytji grabbed me: "*Wai?* What happened?" I told him about the *mamu*.

Next morning, we got up. Looking around. Tjiḻpi Kanytji found the pile of wood. "Oh, son. We've been sleeping next to a grave, somebody's grave." I think he said it was his *tjamu*, one of his grandfathers. "We better go," he said. So we just rolled up our blankets and went. Then he said: "So, that's what you dreamed last night. You might get a bit sick, son." It was a cold morning, that morning. We walked along, made a fire, got warm. Then walked, made a fire. Like that. And I was vomiting all the way to Wallatina.

We arrived in the morning, before lunch. He told the story to my *katja*, poor old thing, Witapitjanu. He was an important *ngangkari*, one of our doctors. A very, very clever *ngangkari*. He'd put his hand on your sick body, and then get a red coal from the fire, rub it in his hands, put it in his mouth, and swallow it. I watched him and I never saw it going past his mouth, behind him, nothing. Always right down. I thought he was making out, but he did it every time. He's the only *ngangkari* I saw do that.

He worked on me. Felt around my body and got something out. Then he felt my *kurun* (white people might say "spirit"). *Kurun*: that's what keeps us alive. You know, that's why I'm doing this book, because I got a *kurun*. Only mine wasn't there. So he walked the way we came in that morning, and he found it by the base of a tree. He got it, brought it back and put it in my heart. In the afternoon I was playing with the kids again. And that was the end of our little trip to Malu Walpa.

* * *

There were people coming and going through our camp all the time. Sometimes people from Mimili or Granite Downs or other places would arrive and stay a while. When they first arrive, they'll make a camp some distance away, where people from our camp can see them. One of our men gets a billycan of water and takes it over to where they're sitting, walking sort of sideways. He puts the billycan on the ground, comes away a few feet and sits down. One of the visitors gets up, picks up the billycan of water, takes a drink and passes it around. Then Kanytji comes up and they talk to him. They might tell him their names; or he might recognise them. Then he'll come back and tell our camp who they are. After that, we might give meat to them or damper. They camp there that night, and come a little closer every day until they're part of the community. Then they might say, "We've got *inma* with us." And they'll dance and sing, and people at Wallatina would watch and learn about it. Then people would sing *inma* from the country around Wallatina, and they'd watch. Somebody would invite them over then, and they

26

would mix with Wallatina people, dancing and singing together.

People speaking other languages, like old Secretary and Tommy Dodd and their families, would come through too. I think Secretary was Kaytetye, from country north of Alice Springs, and Tommy Dodd was Arrernte. They looked different, tall and big men, different from our mob. They could speak Yankunytjatjara too. And they had their own *inma*, dancing their own way. Flash buggers. They might give it to people here if they learn it well.

Sometimes whitefellas would come to Wallatina, but they would only go to see Tommy Cullinan. I only remember one who came to the camp, and that was Mr MacDougall. When he came he was on patrol, but I didn't know what he was doing. He'd only talk to the big people. I only found out years later that he was working for Woomera Rocket Range. I didn't know then that he was coming about the atomic weapons tests the army was doing south of us.

We used to travel a lot, always on the move, especially in winter. We'd go west of Wallatina for dingo scalps, through Watjunya and Atjirikitikititjaranya, right up to Uluṟu. And we'd get dingo pups, beautiful little dogs. I'd cook them and leave them overnight. I like them best next morning when they're cold. Baby dingo. Lovely.

We used to go up and down to Mimili quite a bit, too. That was Tjiḻpi Kanytji's country. They'd go to see relatives and to get *mingku* and *urtjan*. There's no *urtjan* around Wallatina, you can only make rubbish spears from mulga. Sometimes almost everybody in the camp would go, leave Tjiḻpi Tommy Cullinan and his wife behind. He said it'd be all right. I think maybe one or two might have stayed with them to look after his goats.

From Wallatina we'd walk to Pantalytjara, Mulytjantu, Watju. From Watju we turned somehow. There was plenty of bush tucker along the way; the flour, tea and sugar was gone in a couple days. Once, at Watju, an interesting thing happened. Well, interesting for us kids. It started raining during the night, a slow, steady rain. Next morning the older people said that we couldn't travel. So they made the biggest *kaṉku*, just sticks and leaves and more sticks and leaves. And it was really dark inside, but dry and warm.

All day and all night it rained steady. Next day was sunshine so we travelled. There was maybe twenty people altogether. I knew which way they had to go, where the water points are. But there are no worries after the rain, the rockholes and claypans are full. And the ground was soft, easy for walking. As we were going along, they'd tell us kids where that old *ngintaka* went with the *tjiwa* in his tail and the names he gave to the places. Just to the south was that *malu tjina* going east to Wallatina with that euro and their uncle the nightjar. Teaching us the country. Big happy family it was. Plenty of food and it was really good. I didn't even notice how long it took us to get there. We were just playing all the way.

We sat down at Mimili for a while, camped a long way from the homestead. Mimili was called Everard Park then, a cattle station owned by Mr Brady. There were a lot of people, a lot of boys and girls. We were shy for a while, but then we started playing with them. I'd been to Mimili before. I think we might've walked all the way back to Wallatina three or four times. (When Tommy Cullinan sent a telegram saying he needed Tjilpi Kanytji for work, we would catch the mail truck going to Wallatina on its way back to Oodnadatta. That was quick.)

* * *

There was a time, I remember, when we all left Wallatina for business. We walked to Wantjapila, on Granite Downs Station. They had sent a *tjitji ulpuru* to Ernabella. And that *ulpuru* was Teddy Edwards, same fella I seen at Wintinna when I was younger. They sent them on foot, of course. Today they still have that *ulpuru* business, but they sometimes send that boy in a plane, and they always travel with motor cars and trucks.

We walked to Wantjipila and met up with the others. There were so many people! They had a camel team pulling a wagon, and others just had camels and saddles. And there were some

28

pack horses too. Then we started moving slowly up the creek to Iwantja, near Indulkana community there now. I used to take food, billycan of tea and damper, to the *nyiinka* camp. We travelled north from Mengersons Well, to that creek they call Ilintjitjara. All the men and other women went on to meet some people who were coming from Ernabella. I found out later they had a big camp at Lennon Swamp and finished the business there. But there was another time I was part of the business, and I'll talk about that later.

When we got back to Mengersons Well, there was my *tjamu* sitting there. He was the grandfather who gave me my name when I was a baby. My other name, Yami, came from my mother and father. My *tjamu* used to say to me: "Grandson, I gave you my name, when you were a baby. It was Tjiripingka." I think it's from the English words, three fingers, but we couldn't pronounce it that way. He had only three fingers on one hand. When you're a little baby, they get hold of you and press you against their stomach, so you will grow strong like him. He gave me his name, because he loved his grandson. And he used to talk funny, like his mouth was swollen or his tongue was too big. Even today, when my mothers are having fun, happy to see me, they'll talk in a voice like my grandfather and say, "Hey, isn't that our father coming this way?" So I was known as Tjiripingka all that time. I'm Tjiripingka now.

I was getting older, getting ideas. Kelly, they put him through, made him a *nyiinka*, and I lost him for a while. I was still *tjitji kuya-kuya*, a cheeky little kid, not worth worrying about. When I was maybe ten or eleven the Cullinans gave me a job: taking care of the nanny-goats. They had a lot of them; it was their main meat. They ate bullock sometimes, and at Christmas Tjilpi Cullinan would drop two of them, one for us at the camp and one for him. Anyway, I'd yard them up, catch all the kiddykiddy (the little ones), chuck them in the little round yard away from the mothers. Then I'd milk them. My work, and I thought it was pretty good, working. Only milking goats, but I thought it was important. So I'd take the bucket and fill it up with milk and take it to Mrs Cullinan. The women working at the house, Kukika and Kanginy, would already have a fire going, so I'd have my breakfast there.

Next I'd go round to the front door and one of the women would have a white bag with my lunch all ready. Then I'd open the yard gate then and let the buggers go! First I let out the little kiddies, so they'd find their mothers, then I'd open the main gate. Out that way to the south of the homestead, me and the nanny-goats. All the other kids would follow me with little billy-cans or jam tins. Looking to get some milk. Oh, I was a good shepherd.

Sometimes Tjilpi Kanytji would come by, and he'd say to me: "I just couldn't find any kangaroo today. Nothing." Oh, shit. So I round them up, and he'll start breaking branches from young mulga trees. All the nanny-goats would come around and have a feed then. He'll stand there and watch them, saying, "Hum, let me see... Maybe this one. Or maybe this one." He'd grab him and break his neck. "Yes, very nice," he'd say. He'd cut him up and all that. I'd go back later and cover it up.

About midday, when it got a bit warm, the goats would settle down in the shade under the trees. I'd make a fire and put on the billy. The other kids would start milking the goats then, and they'd boil their milk while I'm boiling my tea. We'd break up half a loaf of bread and have a little bit of meat. Sometimes they'd have a rabbit. Me and the kids and the nanny-goats, sitting out there having our dinner.

One day I was looking after the goats a long way out. All the women were there too, about six or seven of them. They'd been looking for rabbit all day, but there wasn't much that way. My mother, Pingkai, came up to me and said: "Hey, son. No rabbits." "Oh, I see," I'd say. Then they did the same trick as Kanytji. They'd grab one of the goats, twist the neck, cut it up, and start to cook it out in the open country. Not many trees around there. So I was standing and watching them and they're eating and... blow me down! Old Tommy Cullinan was coming along in the jeep, on his way to Wallatina Waterhole. He saw me, so he came over, stopped and talked, gave me an orange. And I was thinking all the time: "Oh, shit. He might see the smoke." My mother and everybody were just having the biggest barbecue. But he didn't see it. It was like that a lot of times. Sometimes they would just go in the yard at night and carry away one of the goats. Tjilpi Cullinan never said anything. But I reckon he knew.

Early that winter, Mr and Mrs Cullinan came to the camp wanting to talk to me. They told Kanytji they were going to the Oodnadatta races. Kanytji interpreted for me. He said, "You stay here and look after the nanny-goats." Somebody had to watch them because it was the time when the little nanny-goats were being born. "You look after them and they're gonna bring you back nice things from Oodnadatta." I really wanted to go to the races with them, but I said, "That's all right, I'll look after them." When they got back, they gave me nice shorts, shirt, and shoes with buckles; they looked like girl's shoes, I think. And a towel, soap and fruit. Just gave it to me for looking after those little kiddykiddy. Tjilpi Cullinan asked, "Any little kiddykiddies?" And I said, "Oh, too many, *tjilpi*." And he came to the yard with me and had a look. "Kiddykiddykiddykiddy."

I think I saw through one winter looking after the nanny-goats. Then Tjilpi Kanytji taught me to ride a horse bareback. First he'd lead me around and then, right, I'd try it by myself. And he'd teach me how to shoe the horses. I thought it was good, learning new things. I used to take Tjilpi Cullinan's camp horse to Wallatina Waterhole and he'd drive his truck. Big black horse it was, beautiful. And he'd drive his truck like it was a four-wheel drive.

Once I went to Granite Downs with Kelly and Tjilpi Kanytji. Uncle Harry usually went, but I don't know where he was. They were mustering, and Mr Cullinan sent us to see if there were any Wallatina cattle mixed up with the rest. His brand was "X22". So while they were mustering, we mustered with them. Brought some cattle back.

Then things suddenly changed for me, for all of us at Wallatina. One morning when we were in the camp we felt the ground shake and then afterwards, I can't remember how long, this thing came over us — like a black smoke or a mist. The older people said they'd never seen anything like it before. Soon afterwards there was sickness in the camp. One of my uncles was pretty bad: he had sort of blisters all over his body, and he never got better. There was no clinic at Wallatina. So they took him off to try and get help for him. But he died there, while they were waiting.

It was a real sad time for us. After that, me and my mother and Kanytji and brothers, along with a lot of other people, moved to Mimili. After a while, some people went back to Wallatina. But from that time, we never did. Next time I was there was when I was doing stock work on Granite Downs.

It wasn't unusual to move away from the camp when there's a death. They do that because if they stayed in one place, the hills, trees, everything there reminds them of what happened. And they'd get rid of that person's personal possessions, and those of his close relatives. They just try to forget all about it. You couldn't even say that person's name after that. Other people with the same name, you'd just call *kunmaṉara*. That's the end of the story.

So I didn't think about it for a long time. Never mentioned it to anyone. I don't know what sort of illness it was, and I still don't know. But it stayed in my mind somewhere. I only thought about it years later, that maybe what happened to my uncle had something to do with what happened to my eyesight.

mama – father

kangkaṟu – elder sister

ngangkaṟi – healer, traditional doctor

untal – daughter

katja – son

kami – grandmother

nyiiṉka, – a boy in the stage of seclusion preceding the ceremony that will make him a man

tjitji ulpuru – a boy in ceremony stage

tjamu – grandfather

tjilpi – old man, elder

palya – OK

ngintaka – perentie lizard

tjati – small lizards

kanyala – euro

tjutiny – throwing stick, club

tjitji – child, children

tjuu – buddy, pal

tjïwa – grinding stone

wati – man

ngangkarpa – exclamation, heck

inma – traditional songs and dance

wira – bowls

kanku – shelter

kungka umari – mother-in-law

maku – witchety grubs

ili – wild fig

watarka – umbrella bush

walkal – emu poison bush

tjuntala – colony wattle

kungka tjuta – the women

mai – vegetable food

kampurara – desert rain

ngintaka inma – songs about the perentie

malu – red kangaroo

tawal-tawal – wild gooseberry

tjuni – the insides

wapar, waparitja – 'dreaming', law

urtjan – special wood for making spears, spearwood tree

paiya, wai – exclamations

katja – male relative

mingkul – bush tobacco

malu tjina – kangaroo tracks

tjitji kuya-kuya – ordinary kid

Mimili

Everard Park, that's the whitefella name for it. We call it Mimili, after that place, Piramiminya, close to the homestead. At that time, Mr Brady was gone and the station was owned by the Ponder brothers, three of them, and their partner, David Joseland. All of them were single. There was an old fella too, Fred Moke. He was their cattle adviser. The women in the camp would work in the homestead for them, do the laundry, clean the house, milk the cows, look after the chooks. To me, I reckon those fellas were good. And there was a big camp of Anangu, just south of the homestead, near the foothills by a small sandhill. I wasn't a stranger, of course. I knew some of the people there from before.

Soon after we arrived from Wallatina, a lot of people moved in from Ernabella, the Presbyterian Mission in the Musgrave Ranges. I remember my uncle Treacle was there too. Mimili people had *inma nyuwana*, this new song that someone made up, what they call *inma witini*. They call it that because it was given to somebody at night by one of those *ampaka* that I mentioned before. Gives it to that person when he's asleep – or might be a woman – and he can see that *ampaka* dancing, hear him singing. They get it then, memorise it, and teach the others. This one's a song about the places around Mimili and what happened there. Lively, dancing song, and I can still sing it.

I don't know how many days or weeks they were doing that. But after a while we left the *inma*, and travelled west with some other people on camels. To Victory Well, through the ranges, past that *walawuru* nest, that eaglehawk *wapar*.

I didn't know the country around Mimili very well, but Tjilpi Kanytji taught me some things about it. He didn't set out to teach me like a TAFE course, paid by the Department of

34

Employment, Education and Training. It just came natural to him. He told me that this was his country, he was *kanytjil* and *tjalku*, a rabbit-eared bandicoot man. He said all the *tjalku* started from Mintabie on their way to Mimili. He told me about *walpuṭi*, the banded ant-eater *wapar*. He taught me about the songlines, or as much as he could tell a kid. He told me where the water points were. He told me about his mother, my *kami*, but I can't remember seeing her. And he showed me where he was born.

So I listened to him as we travelled along. Then we stopped, and the rain came. And it rained and rained. We just had this *kaṇku*, made of sticks and spinifex and I think some canvas. But mainly sticks. It just kept on raining, so Johnny Wangin and Pipai, two *wati tawariṭja*, decided to take some of the kids back to Mimili. So I went with them. I left my mother and father there, along with the others, standing in the rain.

I think we had one camel to carry the wet blankets. After walking most of the day in the rain, the two men said to us, "You kids wait here. We'll take the two dogs and go look for *maḻu*." It started getting late then, getting dark. I was worried. I was with the other kids, but I was worried myself. We had a little fire and it was growing brighter as it got darker. I was thinking: "Gee, I hope those two men come back. I'm really scared now. Who knows what might happen?" Well, after a while they did turn up and they had a *maḻu* with them. So they made a big fire, dug a hole for the *maḻu*, and cooked it there beside a mulga tree. We slept around that big fire, trying to make sort of a shelter. But it was steady rain. Next morning we just walked; we just wanted to get back to Mimili.

Back at the main camp, I stayed with one of my older brothers (I can't say his name because he's passed away now) and my age-mate, Peter Mungkari. My mother and father were still out there somewhere with the others. One was *nyiiṇka*; me and Peter were what they call *tjitji kungkatja*. We'd go out hunting together. One time this older fella, a *wati*, took the three of us and that *nyiiṇka* hunting in the hills around Mimili. He was a good bloke, good with kids. He'd take them out bush all the time. We walked north-west of the homestead, looking for *kanyaḻa*. And that *nyiiṉka* and that *wati* made me and Peter Mungkari climb up just about every rock in Mimili. Trying to hunt out the *kanyaḻa* and drive them towards the other two waiting around the other side. When we'd get down, they'd say, "One came past here all right, but we missed it." I could see the blade of his spear was broken. And then the old fella would say, "Just one more, can you try that hill over there?" I think he really wanted some meat. There wasn't much around at Mimili that time. "Aaah, come on, Uncle. No, we're tired." "Don't give me that. *Tjiṯji awai!* Let's go, you kids." But they got nothing. That night we camped, no blankets and nothing to eat. Just a little drink of water from the rockhole.

Next morning this *wati* said, "All right. We might try the scrub for kangaroo. *Ngawaririnyi*." This is where two of us walk straight through the bush, and the men with spears run along on an angle. If we frighten some kangaroo, they might run into the others. But it didn't work. So he said to us two kids: "Right. Start climbing. First we'll try that hill over there." So we did, and we were getting real hungry by then. But we were lucky, they got one. They just cooked it right there: *kanyaḻa ngunytju*. And we had the biggest feed. All of us were the same. I just didn't want to move.

There was another thing we did. I wasn't sure if I should put it in the book, but one night we decided to pinch some oranges from Everard Park Homestead. Three of us went: that *nyiiṉka* again, Peter Mungkari and me. They told me to wait outside the yard. I had this white flour bag, and they chucked them over the fence to me. Lights were on in the homestead. I could hear the whitefellas talking, but I couldn't understand what they were saying. Anyway, we filled up the bag, and we walked all the way to the *nyiiṉka* camp. Got the oranges out. I looked: "Hey, funny-shaped oranges." *Wiya*, they were lemons! So we cooked them in the warm earth. We ate them that way, but they made my teeth go funny. OK, "No more pinching oranges, that's it."

I was getting homesick for Wallatina. It had everything. And there was just not much at Mimili. Then a lot of people came into the camp, and my mother and Kanytji got back from wherever they'd been. They had some dingo scalps, so they got plenty of tucker from the Ponder brothers, and it was good for a while. Kanytji and his brother got a job at the station then, contract work building a stockyard at Gap Swamp, near the well there. Me and one of my elder brothers, Andy Pungkai, went with them. They had two camels and a wagon, swinging axes, cutting posts. And me and Andy, he was a *nyiinka*, we just went hunting with the dogs everyday, bringing in the kangaroo.

The Ponder brothers and David Joseland were mustering the biggest mob of horses. They had a lot of unbroken horses in the yard, ready for branding, so I went over with the other boys: Hughie Tjami and Mike Tapaya, they were almost *nyiinka*, and another age-mate of mine, Bruce Stanley. And the Ponder brothers gave us the job of cutting out the colts and helping with the branding. I thought I was pretty good, no worries. It needed a few of us to do the job: one fella with a lasso, or head rope; one with a hind-leg rope; and one with a foreleg rope. The one with the rope around the horse's foreleg would drop him, then they'd hold him down and brand him with a hot iron. If it was a filly, they'd just brand it and put it into another yard, but they gelded the stallions. I'd hold onto the leg rope while they were branding. I had to give it a bit of slack, and when somebody said "OK", I'd let go. He just said "OK" so I thought that was David Joseland's name: "OK Akainya." And that's what we started calling him: "Oh, right, Akainya" or "Hey, Akainya's coming." I was pretty smart, you know. I'd worked out his name.

And they paid us pretty well with a big billycan of tea and plenty to eat on a big tray. We had the biggest feed doing that job. And they dressed us up, gave us all shirts and riding trousers. I think the trousers were for girls, because they had no fly, so they looked the same front and back. Had numbers on them too. I don't know what that was for. We used to laugh about it: "Hey, look at that kid over there. What is he, looking the other way or facing us?" We opened them up anyway with a piece of broken glass and just left them open, you know, for emergencies. And we had these funny shoes or boots. Bruce Stanley got a rasp and tried to make his like R. M. Williams's

Cuban-heel riding boots. But it didn't work – he made the heel too skinny. So when he put them on, the front was bigger than the back and they looked funny.

So that was my first work on the station. We stayed around the camp, thinking we might get other work. After a while, they started branding cattle in the homestead yard. Me and Bruce Stanley went over and just stood around, watching. Kanytji and the others were in the yard with the cattle. Sandy Ponder came up and started talking to us. Kanytji heard him and told us, "He's asking you if you want to work." Did we!

I already knew how to ride a horse from Wallatina, and they were going out mustering at Park Well, east of the homestead. So me and Bruce went with them. After we drafted the cattle out, they started branding. I was helping to throw the calves down, and they were saying: "Come on, you gotta throw that calf. Train your muscles. Let's see how strong you are." And all that. Then they cut the young bulls' balls, took them and chucked them in the barbecue. They gave me some and said, "That's for your muscles." And I thought, "Oh, yeah, well that must be right." And every branding time I used to look forward to eating the balls. It's not bad either. Sometimes the cook would take them, chuck them in the pot and make a curry.

Then they went out to muster the working horses again. I can still see Tjilpi Kanytji wearing his white hat with a black hatband, and he really looked the part. Proper stockman. Me, Bruce and Kanytji split from the horse-tailers, who left the main party and carried on to the camp at Gap Well where we met up with them later. We went around that black hill there and saw a lot of tracks made by Anangu. Then we saw this small kanga-roo. Now, they tell you not to gallop a horse, but we chased it anyway. Kanytji got to it first, killed it with a stick, picked it up and put it across his saddle. When we got close to the camp, he put the kangaroo in the bushes for later. When we got to the stockyard close to the well, the Ponder brothers and some other stockmen were already there with cattle. We yarded the cattle and made a camp. After we unsaddled our horses, they'd come up and give us a pannikin and tell us to pour water on the horses' backs. We had to give the horses a little bit of a wash to take off the sweat and salt, hobble them up then and let them go. Then the cook gave us beef and damper, and some more damper with golden syrup. That's all we had, but the white people would have more. When we had finished, we went back to where we dropped that kangaroo and cooked it and had a big party.

I remember a lot of Anangu were missing, that must've been the tracks we saw by the black hill. Probably moved out somewhere on business. The workers stayed behind: me, that *nyiinka*, Peter Mungkari, and some of the men. There was a lot of whitefellas working too. We went out with packhorses through Ronalds Well and Bettys Well. Camped there the first night. Then next morning we travelled west of Ngalyatjalinynga. And we had these rough horses. They brought them from Tieyon, and we took them out just after they broke them in. Real wild buggers. That morning Peter Mungkari got this blue horse. It threw him three times! After the last time he got another horse, caught the blue one, unsaddled it, and just let it go. We went right up to a place north of Pocket Well, where there was a waterhole. We had to get water in a bucket and pour it into a hole we dug in the ground lined with double canvas for the horses to drink.

So, while they're watering their horses, I was riding bareback on this good working horse, rounding up the rest of them. They started to gallop away, so I got alongside to wheel them around. Then they pulled up quick, and my horse just stopped. I kept going, right over his head! The others saw me lying in the dirt and laughed.

Next morning the horse-tailers brought the horses to the camp. We caught our favourite ones and went mustering cattle back to Bettys Well. We split up in pairs. I went with Wally Ponder. He was riding this brown horse, very touchy. And I was on a young and lively bay mare. But we didn't see any tracks, and we didn't know where the others were. So Wally Ponder took out a tin of wax matches they used to have, struck a match, and dropped it on some spinifex. Sent a big smoke. He decided to go back to Bettys Well, and on the way there we saw a few cattle sleeping in the shade. They bolted when they saw us, and Wally Ponder took off on this fast, toey horse. Flat out. I watched him spin them around, and we talked to them then, quietened them down. Back at Bettys Well, those other musterers were bringing cattle in. I could see a big mob on the left and a big mob on the right. After lunch, they told me and two others to tail the mob, keep them together, and they went out to look for more. That afternoon they came back with more cattle, put them with our mob, and I think they galloped to the camp for a drink of tea. Then we yarded the lot.

As we were taking them across the creek to the yard I saw this young teenager sitting on a rock, a horse standing alongside. He was all dressed in blue and he had a whip in his hand. I stared at him and I thought, "Gee, he's a smart fella!" Then he came up and joined us, yarding the cattle. When a cow or steer broke away from the mob, he just took off, cracking his whip and wheeling them around. "Gee," I said. "Who's this bloke? He's a stranger, this fella." So we yard them up, talk to them, and I recognised him then. It was Wallace Wallatina. He used to be at Wallatina, but he was working for Granite Downs now. All dressed up in blue! I said: "Hey, brother! Brother, *wai? Wai? WAI? Nyuntu palya?* Hey, how are you?" I just couldn't recognise you." He looked fantastic.

That night, me and Wallace got back to the camp, watered our horses, unsaddled them, washed them down, and hobbled them out. We got out our quart pots and had a drink of tea. It was a quiet night and in the distance somewhere, I could hear the Condamine bells on the horses: dong dong dong. I loved listening to those bells. There's a nice, sandy creek at Bettys Well, and I was just lying back on my swag, looking off at the gum trees.

I think it was the next day when I heard a mob of packhorses coming, and I saw a whitefella riding up lead, a couple of Anangu and some other whitefellas behind. It was Brian Norris from Kenmore. Kenmore Park was the station north of Mimili and it was owned by Ron Norris. His brother, Brian, was the head stockman. They were all coming to get their cattle. There were no fences between the stations in those days and the cattle just wandered around because it was open country.

There was a big stock camp then, stockmen and horses from Kenmore, Granite Downs, and Mimili. Every day they'd go mustering, and I stayed behind, a long way from the stock camp, tailing a mob of cattle with Joe Peters, an uncle of mine from Kenmore, and a bloke from Granite Downs. Horse-tailers from Mimili and Kenmore were there too, back at the camp, and the cook, making damper and boiling beef. We looked after cattle all day, making sure they didn't wander off. We'd let them feed, and we'd walk around, sit on a horse, leg across the saddle, roll a cigarette, chase flies, blow smoke. That's how it was. If we got off the horse and sat on the ground, the boss didn't like it. He'd come and tell you off: "Get your faahking arse off the ground!" Yeah. We could get off our horses only when the cattle settle down, sleeping in the shade.

After they finished mustering out from Bettys Well, we started cutting the cattle out on the flat. Cattle were there in one mob, might be five hundred or a thousand head, and it was fantastic. There was dust everywhere, and people calling out over the noise of the cattle. Whips were cracking, bosses growling at us. All around the cattle there were stockmen on horses, keeping them boxed in. Three people go into the mob on camp horses then: a Mimili bloke, one of the Ponder brothers, or Dave Joseland; Tommy Singer from Granite Downs; and Brian Norris from Kenmore Park. Boss man goes in to see their own cattle, looking for the brand.

To start off they'll cut out a small, mixed-up mob of cattle: bullocks, cows and calves. One stockman would hold them. They'd be what they call coachers. There'd be enough room between those few cattle and the big mob for maybe six men on horses, and they'd be what they call "facing the camp". That is, facing the bosses on their camp horses inside the main mob. One of those blokes inside the mob would drop his whip on the one he wanted to come out. And the camp horses they had! Soon as he touched one with his whip, that horse would wheel

41

him out. They could turn on a sixpence, and if he wasn't careful he could fall off. Camp horse wouldn't care, it just wanted that bullock. Then one of those stockmen facing the camp would take that steer or bullock or one of the cattle from the other station and turn it to that mob of coachers.

Sometimes one would come out of the main mob by mistake and the boss man might call out, "Cut the red one back and let the bully one go," or something like that. If there's a big mob of cattle, we'd work all day until all that was left in the main mob were the Everard cows and calves. We'd try to finish cutting out by lunch time so we could yard the cows and calves and brand the cleanskins before dark. Then we'd let them go and yard the other cattle for the night. That's what we tried to do, but it didn't always work that way.

When we'd finished mustering around Bettys Well, we'd move the whole camp with the cattle – Everard fat cattle for trucking and their cattle from Kenmore and Granite Downs – to the next watering point, Victory Well. So they'd muster out from there for a couple of days, and we'd draft out the cows and calves from Everard Park and move on again with the mob. We'd do this until we went to all the watering points on Everard Park. It's what they called tender muster.

I liked it, I liked the stock work. And what I liked about it was riding horses. That's all. The work might've been important, but what was important to me was riding the horses. I used to love yarding time, when they bring the cattle into the yard. Sometimes one of them, a cow or bullock, might break away, and I loved chasing it, wheeling it around, and bringing it back to the mob. Or when a little cleanskin broke away, I couldn't bring them back to the yard like the older ones, they'd tell me to jump off the horse and throw it down. And I loved that. When I got a bit more experienced I was able to do those things. But at Mimili I was a bit of a jackeroo, just learning. Still doing my apprenticeship.

I never worried about the long hours. I suppose I was a little bit mad, but no different from the other young fellas. All I wanted to do when I woke up was ride horses. Ride the whitefellas' horses and make them gallop. When I had learnt a bit more, the rougher the horses they gave me, the more I loved it. I wasn't cruel, but if they got rough, I got rough with them too. Of course, there's no money in the saddle. No money at all. I found that out later. But then the only thing I thought about was the horses.

After they finished mustering, we had what they called a cut-out camp. Granite Downs got their cattle, Kenmore Park drafted out theirs, like that. We drafted out the fat Mimili bullocks for trucking. We didn't put them on trucks then, but would walk them to the railhead at Finke. The afternoon before we started, we'd water the cattle. Because there were so many, we had to break them up. Water one mob first and, when they had enough, push them out of the way and bring in another lot. We'd be at the back, long way back, still holding the mob. "Aaaaaah. Blaaaaaaah." They'd be carrying on.

After they'd gone with their cattle back to Kenmore and Granite Downs, we stayed behind and got the fat bullocks ready to go. There might've been eleven or twelve hundred head and they were walking them to the railhead at Finke. Me, Bruce Stanley, Andy Pungkai, and old Fred Moke started taking them to Dinnertime Well. Because they were all bullocks, they were a bit quicker than cows and calves.

It was afternoon. They were all lying down, and me and Fred Moke were watching. We were in the saddle, he's rolling a cigarette and having a yarn. I didn't really understand what he was talking about. But I had a smile. We heard something coming then, and saw the big red truck from Ernabella. There was a group of people on the back. So he started off: "Chck, chck, chck." And soon he was at full gallop, cracking his whip. I started after him. We got close enough to the truck for the people in the back to see us, but they didn't say anything to the driver. I don't know why we were trying to catch him. Maybe Fred wanted to give a message to the Mimili homestead. But I knew who it was in that truck now. It was Ron Trudinger, the Ernabella missionary, and in the back was my future wife, Lucy. She told me years later that she remembered seeing two white-

43

fellas on horses chasing the Ernabella truck. "Two whitefellas!" I said. "What!" And she told me what year that was. It was 1954.

Me and Fred went back to the stock camp and had dinner. Then Dave Joseland and some others arrived with packhorses. That afternoon they started walking the cattle to Finke. Fred Moke told me and Andy Pungkai that we weren't going, so we went back to Mimili. We cut the neck strap on the horses and let them out in the paddock. Our work was finished.

There still wasn't many Anangu around. Kanytji and the rest of them were still on business at Granite Downs. His brother stayed behind and he was sitting down at Carmeena Bore with his wife, looking after the engine, pumping water. And there was me and Andy. We didn't sit down for long. Fred Moke told us: "Righto! We gotta stockyard to build." This time they had two machines: one was a saw on two wheels that they pushed along, and the other was a post-hole digger. Me and Andy Pungkai had to get the timber that some Anangu had already cut and heaped up near Pigeon Bore. We had a wagon and two camels. The Ponder brothers had marked out the yard on the ground with pegs and string, where the different drafting rooms would be, the race and the gates. They made a base for the gate: cement in a bucket, put a fruit tin in the centre, and the gate post would go in there to make it swing. And while they were doing this, I was taking notice. I was still a jackeroo. Didn't know much, but I was learning.

When we finished carting the timbers, we started putting them in the ground. They put me on with Fred Moke. He operated the machine that dug the holes, and my job was to get the dirt out with this special, curved shovel. Ponder brothers would be pulling that saw, cutting the posts, putting them in the ground. They were really hard workers. If you go to Robbs Well today, you'll see the kind of posts they put in. They're huge! Hard workers, those boys.

They had this old cook working there, German fella. His name was Mick Mitchelburk. He always used to keep a knife under his pillow at night. He told me a *kutatji* might be coming.

He had a name for him too, but I forget what it was. But he knew, and he was frightened of them. He was a funny bloke. He lived in a little tin shed by himself.

One morning, while we were finishing the yard, I got up and went to get the two camels. I was always the first to get up. I went east of the homestead following their track. When I found them, I had to undo their hobbles. I never liked the black one, the big bull called Mantjuluna. He always gave me a funny look. The other one, Mitchelburk, was an old bullock and he was lovely, nice and quiet. Kanytji's brother always told me to be careful with bull camels. When I squatted to undo the hobble strap, I had to be ready to jump. Always undo the near strap and tie it on the off-side, he said. If you start with the strap on the far side, he might hit you with the hobble chain still tied to other leg. So I took special notice of what he said. I'd just let that black one walk along with the hobbles still tied to his far side (fuck him!), then led him along on his noseline so the other camel would follow. But, gee, they were smart camels. They could really pull that wagon full of heavy timbers. Sometimes, when they went a bit lazy, Andy'd get up on the wagon and make a noise like he had a whip: "Come on! Pull, ya bastard." And he'd just make them go.

Anyway, this morning I brought the camels in, and my brother Andy was cutting wood for the kitchen. I went inside the tin shed there, having breakfast, when I heard this truck coming. It was that red Ernabella truck coming back. Turns out they'd been to Adelaide to see the Queen. Behind the truck's cabin were a couple of big cupboards with clothes for the people in them. All the young women were in the back, sitting near the cabin, and behind them were the men sitting close to the tail-gate. When they pulled up, Andy, because he's a *nyiinka* and girls can't see him, runs off and hides. Didn't matter for me, I was still a kid, but I just stayed in the shed and hid too. Looking through a little hole in the sheet of iron. I was thinking, "Gee, I wish I could go with them."

Anyway, two whitefellas and one white woman got out of the truck and went inside the homestead, talking to the Ponder brothers and old Mitchelburk. I suppose they were having a cup of tea and cake. I finished my breakfast and just sat there, looking out. When they came out, Wally Ponder got on the truck. He sat down in the back with the men. He was carrying a cattle prod, and I figured he was going to Ernabella or Kenmore to catch the mail truck to Finke so he could help out the others trucking the fat bullocks.

Other times I remember working with Mitchelburk. "Come on, *wiyai*," he would say, "we're going to do some gardening." So I would work with him doing garden work. I used to push around the wheelbarrow with the horse shit and cow shit, unloading it onto the beds. He was growing some tomatoes and potatoes, onions and lettuce. One of my other duties was to feed the chooks, collect the eggs, and take them to him. And I'd go after the cows in the evening, bring them in, separate the calf from the old cow. I think the women working in the homestead milked her. In the morning, I'd open the gate for the cows and the chooks. Then I'd go and cut wood for the kitchen. Mitchelburk had a fire going all the time, and I was getting sick of cutting wood for him.

One day the men came back from Finke. Bruce Stanley and the others had got nice things from the Finke store. You know, riding clothes and everything. And they looked smart. Dave Joseland and Andy Pungkai went to round up a killer. They brought in a few cattle, and there was a stray among the Mimili mob: one big, white-faced steer with the Kenmore brand. While they were yarding it, they heard this car coming (Andy told me this later). It was Ron Norris from Kenmore Park in a red ute. When Joseland saw the car he said, "Oh, shit." Ron Norris went inside the homestead to talk to the Ponder brothers. Then Dave Joseland unsaddled his horse and walked back to the house. We didn't know what was going on, so we just sat there waiting for supper. Then we saw those whitefellas walking past us to the stockyard, to see the cattle. They had a real good look, then they went back in the house again. I didn't hear Ron Norris leave until late. Early in the morning, before the sun was up, the Ponder brothers went to the yard and dropped the killer. One big, white-faced steer. The one with the Kenmore brand.

I was still working with Mitchelburk in the garden. Andy Pungkai was still around doing something else. I said to Andy, "Hey, this old whitefella is no good, you know?" So one day, you know what he did to me? There were clouds coming up, and it really looked like rain. Old Mitchelburk told me to get up on the roof to clean the gutters. So after I got up on the roof, he took the ladder away. I reckon he thought I wouldn't do any work, just come down the ladder and go away. I know he never trusted us Aṉangu. And while I was up there, cleaning the gutters, it started to rain – a big thunderstorm. My father's brother was there, and he got the ladder for me. Then he just told Mitchelburk off. He was really wild. When I came down, he was still swearing at him.

I'd had enough. I said to Andy: "Hey, I don't like this Mitchelburk, you know, he keeps giving me shit jobs. I want to ride horses, not all this. I think I'll leave. Tell him to stick it up his arse." By this time, people had come back from business at Granite Downs. There were a lot of people from Ernabella at Mimili, and there were a lot of *nyiiṉka tjuṯa*. They were having business at Mimili then, and I didn't know anything about it. Biggest mob was there: boys, girls, too many. Even Tommy Dodd turned up from somewhere. I remembered seeing him at Wallatina. So I stopped working for Mitchelburk and just stayed in the camp.

We'd go swimming at Robbs Well tank. I never learned how to swim, so I was just hanging on, going around the side of the tank. I was watching everybody diving, so I decided, well, if they're doing it, I might as well get up. So I climbed up on the spill pipe, jumped in, and nearly drowned. Adrian, one of my brothers from Ernabella, got me out. I was vomiting up water. From that afternoon I never went back to that water again. The others could go in but I would just walk around eating *kampuṟara*.

I think they must've finished with the business and Ernabella people went back. They started moving east to Iwantja and I went with them. We were travelling slowly.

Tommy Dodd with his wagon, others with camels. A few days later, when we got to Mengersons Well, Tjilpi Kanytji stopped some white people in a car going towards Mimili. He asked them to ask the Ponder brothers to send over some tea and sugar. And they did. When we got to Iwantja, Tjilpi Kanytji told me to go to the gate on the main track with my brother. He said maybe they left tea and sugar there. And we found a hessian bag with the biggest mob of sugar and tea. He even chucked in a tin of meat. And Kanytji only asked for tea and sugar. I think they might've been a good type of people somehow.

We had a bit of trouble carrying that bag back, it was a bit heavy. When we got to the camp, people from Granite Downs had arrived. That night they had *inma*, you know, everybody singing and dancing. It was a happy time at first. After a little while we moved the camp to Chandler Well. They made Peter Mungkari and another uncle of mine, Norman Patapata, *nyiinka*. The adults told me I had to take tea and damper to them. They were camping away from the others now, of course. So I go out to find them, calling out "*Wai, wai.*" I could hear them tapping the ground with sticks, but there was too much scrub and I couldn't see them. When I got to their camp, I could see they'd been hunting. So they gave me meat, and I gave them tea and damper.

A couple of days later everybody got ready to go to Mimili. We got up early, and everybody was busy packing up their camels and all that. Tjilpi Kanytji was putting the swags on one camel and helping others put their swags on too. My two brothers were standing there, and then I said, "That's it. I'm not going with you." I told my mother: "I'm going east, I'm going to Granite Downs." She started to cry. I told my other brother (not Shannon), that I wasn't coming back to Mimili. Tjilpi Kanytji was there and he kept saying: "*Wai?* What's happening, son?" And I told him, "I'm going east."

So I left with Tommy Brown and his wife, Eileen, my mother's sister. I only saw Kanytji's face with my own eyes twice after that. That's when I was working as a stockman on Granite Downs, before I went blind.

inma nuywana – new song

waḻawuru – wedge-tailed eagle

ampaka – gnome creatures

kanytjil – pig-footed bandicoot

wati tawaritja – young men

tjitji kungkatja – young teenagers

kami – grandmother

nyiiṉka – boy in ceremony stage

kanyaḻa ngunytju – adult female euros

wiya – no

Wai! Nyuntu palya? – Hey! How are you?

kuṯatji – kurdaitcha man

wiyai – boy

nyiiṉka tjuṯa – a lot of bush boys

kampuṟara – desert raisin

Granite Downs

When we got to Granite Downs – it was only half a day's walk from Iwantja – I camped with Tommy Brown and Auntie Eileen Brown for a while. Johnny Cullinan was there. He was *wati tawaritja*, and they'd ask me to take him meat and damper. But I never camped with him. I didn't know much about the place and I wasn't sure.

It was a big camp at Granite Downs, Yankunytjatjara and Pitjantjatjara mixed. It wasn't far from the homestead, just on the other side of a hill to the north, in a beautiful creek. Good country: a lot of firewood and thick scrub of *ngaṯuṉ*.

I'd been there a few days when I decided to go the station homestead. Soon as I get there, this whitefella calls out to me: "Hey, blackfella! Where you from?" I think I said Mimili, or maybe even Wallatina. So he asks me if I want a job.

Turns out he was the owner of Granite Downs, Jim Davey. Well, that was one of the names they used to call him. So he took me into the store and just dressed me up. Gaberdine riding trousers, light blue shirt, riding boots, hat, the whole lot. And I thought, "Hey, now this is all right. So, I'm a working boy now." All dressed up and I'm feeling pretty good.

When I came out, I saw other *wati* there, over by the yard. Biggest mob of men: Whisky, Wangkanya, Alec Baker, Allan Downs, Wallace Wallatina, and some that's passed away now. And Treacle was there. I think they must have just got back from Iwantja, from that business. And I could see boys my age too: Andrew Breaden, Ginger Mofila, and Wallace Wallatina. I was to spend a lot of time with those fellas.

They were drafting out horses. One fella I remember from Mimili, Tommy Singer – he was Jim Davey's nephew – he gets into this round yard. From that, there's all these gates going into different yards. They'd put one horse into the yard, and Tommy Singer'd go around and look at it. He knew every horse's name, and who could ride it. He'd say, "Right, this one's for Whisky, that one's for Wangka." He'd look at another one: "No, unbroken, push 'im out." He'd decide on the camp horses, packhorses, night horses. Put them out in those different yards. As he was doing that, he'd be writing in a big book, counting up the horses, I suppose. Allan Downs was sort of Tommy Singer's right-hand man. He'd put a neck strap on the horses and a hobble, and let them go. The ones they couldn't catch, they put them in the race.

When they put one in the yard that was a little bit over the hill, Tommy Singer would say, "Aaah. This one's for Wallatina Kid." That's me. And he'd give me that one. What a bloke! He spoke all the time in English, but he knew some language. Only he couldn't say *nyanytju*, the word for horse. He'd call them "nandoo". He'd say, "You got any nandoo?" I soon found out he was a lovely man, Tommy Singer.

I found out that we were getting five riding horses. Each. And then there were packhorses, night horses, bronc horses, and camp horses. We had all those. And saddles and riding gear were all supplied. All that belonged to the station, and they told us we had to look after them. Then the young men – Alec Baker and Whisky and the others – started riding their best buckjumpers.

There was this light bay horse called Paddy Way. He had mean eyes, mean pink eyes. He was a mean-looking mongrel. They named him after the old part-Aboriginal bloke who broke him in. He was at Granite Downs too. They said if anybody can handle him, Whisky can. So they caught him, saddled him up, and he's standing there like he's half-asleep. Whisky goes over and gets on. When they let him go, I couldn't believe how that horse bucked. I reckon he was doing figure of eights in mid-air. And Whisky, he just stuck on like... I don't know, like a little monkey. Riding up there and fanning him with his hat. Gee, he was a good rider. Looked like he just knew what that horse was going to do next. I was sitting on the top rail of the stockyard, watching him, and thinking, "Yeah. I'll be like him one day." I really admired him, the way he handled horses. He was an expert. After that, Wangka's horse starts to buck, then it looked like everybody's horse was bucking. All except mine. And just as well, too.

Then we started off for Malu Walpa. We had packhorses, and a big black truck carried other supplies. When we got there, we started mustering. We were all the horse-tailers: Andrew Breaden, Ginger Mofila, Wangka, another fella, Wallace Wallatina, and me. This is what we had to do. Main thing is to get the horses early in the morning and bring them back to the stock camp. We couldn't sit down, couldn't warm our hands on the fire. Horse-tailers have to catch the horses for those cattlemen, and they'll put the bridle and saddle on. Then, when we were finished that, we could stop and sit by the fire, have a drink of tea and breakfast. The best horse-tailers – like Hughie Cullinan – would just know which Granite Downs horses were missing, gone bush. So he'd saddle up and go after them. When the cattlemen go off mustering, horse-tailers stay behind, on a riding horse, and watch the others, make sure they don't wander away too far. When those blokes come back with the cattle, they'd have lunch and change to a fresh horse from the mob we'd been looking after.

Horse-tailers had other jobs too. We had to cart wood on foot for the cook, but we could use a packhorse to carry the canteens of water. Or the cook might want a windbreak, and one of the horse-tailers would have to make him one. Sometimes we'd come in and the cook would still be cooking his damper, and he'd say, "Come on, give me a hand." Getting the camp ovens ready, greasing them and all that. And we'd tell him, "No way, that's your job!" "Come on. Look," he'd say, "I'm struggling here by myself." "Yeah, yeah. Well, that's yours. Faahk you."

Another job during the day, we had to shoe the horses: camp horse, night horse, special horses for different work. Cattle bloke hasn't got time to shoe a horse, so the horse-tailer's got to shoe it for him. Me and Hughie Cullinan used to do that. Sometimes a cattle bloke would bring in a horse and he might have a girth sore. So we'll put medicine on, or we might show Tommy Singer, the head stockman. He might say to that fella, "Now, look, you know, you gotta look after your horse." Anyway, so that's the kind of things the horse-tailers had to do.

So, back at Malu Walpa, we get up early in the morning, what they call piccaninny daylight – when those big stars are coming up – maybe three in the morning. We had to pick up our bridles, walk along, stop and listen for the bells. We knew which horse had which bell: big ones that go "ding, dong, dong" and little ones too. We'd hear them way off in the dark: "tingalingaling". Sounds beautiful. So we'd walk and walk in pairs: me and Wallace, Ginger and Andrew. Four kids. We'd be asking each other in the dark: "*Tjuu, palya*? You OK?" Then we'd hear a bell: "ding ding, dingleding". There they were. So I said, "Oh, yeah, I'll catch this horse. I think he can carry me." Ride him bareback back to the camp. I'm just about to catch him when somebody cracks a whip. They're galloping past us, all those *wati* – Wangka and Whisky and the rest of them. And those horses just bolted. "Hahaha. You *tjitji* gotta walk! Walk back to the camp!" And they just left us there, laughing and cracking their whips. Faahkinell.

People started arriving next morning: Todmorden, Welbourne Hill, Wallatina, Mimili, Kenmore, De Rose Hill, Tieyon. All the stations next door to Granite Downs. It was a big station, Granite Downs. And it was the biggest muster! There was biggest mob of horses, and biggest mob of horse-tailers. It was a happy time, a big happy time. So many horses.

Every station came in with their own truck. And they'd have their own stockmen and cook. And all the white people, they'd be camping separate from each other. They'd all be talking to each other, making plans where they're going to go and what they're going to do. And they'd be working together. But they always camp with their own truck, in their own camp. Anangu, us Aboriginal workers from Granite Downs and the neighbouring stations, we'd all sleep in one mob. There'd be a lot of little fires, and they'll just be talking and laughing together. They'd go to their different bosses, or to the cook to get their food – cut lunch or cut supper. But they'll come back to the camp – our camp, or I don't know who's camp it was, but it was all together. They were just happy, happy to see each other I suppose. They were all relations – *walytja tjuṯa*.

I don't know just when those tender musters stopped. But when we were working on the cattle, other Aṉangu would be working on the fence lines. I think one whitefella was sort of organising them. Mainly they were the sort of people good at swinging an axe, good at cutting posts and clearing the fence line. They were a bit older, I think, and I think they would take their wife and kids with them. The teenagers and young men, single and married, mostly worked with the horses and cattle. I never worked on the fencing. I wasn't any good at it. More fences came in the 1960s, until all the stations had boundary fences.

After the muster at Maḻu Walpa, we moved the camp and took the mob of cattle to other bores on Granite Downs, mustered around those, and when we reached Lambina, east of Granite Downs, they picked up their own cattle to walk them back to their own stations. Then Granite Downs blokes started walking the fat bullocks to Oodnadatta for trucking down to Adelaide. I didn't go for a while; I was still learning. When I was at Mimili I was sort of a jackeroo, but now I thought I was really a ringer. I was doing the work.

And I learned a lot, about mustering and branding and getting fat bullocks ready for trucking. Treacle, Whisky, Alec Baker and, later on, Hughie Cullinan, they were my teachers. And especially Tommy Singer. I'd ride alongside with him, and he'd show me how to ride properly, how to have my legs forward, and all that. And I'd watch him and say, "Oh, right. So that's how you do it." He was a good horseman, good cattleman. And he was really good with kids, really good. Talk to us in a really good way. Sometimes the two of us would go mustering out from the homestead, not far, maybe one or two miles. We'd get off and have a piss. Then the horse would have a piss. And he'd tell us to tighten the girth again. They reckon that when we first caught the horses, they'd have a full tummy. After we rode them for a while, their tummy got sort of loose. So we had to tighten the girth so it wouldn't start rubbing and make a sore under their front legs. So I was learning.

I tried to listen to everything Tommy Singer told me. He taught me about breaking horses. He showed me how to handle them: picking up their feet and touching around the rump, walking them around. Then he'd put shoes on them straight away. Walk them around again with what they call a coacher horse. Next time there's a muster, they'll take those young colts and educate them. But not for long, then they'll go back in the horse paddock for maybe a four-week spell. After that they'd be fresh horses because they know how to work. And that's the time they buck like anything.

When Tommy Singer wasn't around, I used to help this blond-headed mechanic in the workshop. He'd tell me about the tools and I'd hand him over the spare parts he'd ask for. He was very smart. It was the first time I'd seen an engine on the block, not in the car. He'd work on it, then start it up. Stone the crows! I couldn't figure out how it could run without the rest of the car – the seats and wheels and all that. He really knew what he was doing, that fella.

One day we were at the homestead yard breaking in young horses, and these two stockmen rode in from the east. One bloke was a whitefella called Jack Long. The other was Anangu, and his name was Hughie Cullinan. "Now, who's this cowboy?" I'm thinking to myself, looking at Hughie. They'd been out droving cattle, all the way down to Marree country: William Creek, Anna Creek, right down that way. Now they'd come back. Of course, Treacle and Wangka and Whisky and all the young men were pleased to see Hughie. So I'm watching them talking, and I'm thinking, "So, this is the fella." Then he calls me over, "*Tjitji awai!*" He was a proper ringer. Smart.

I never saw much of Jim Davey, the owner. I didn't know much about him then. All we knew was that he was the boss, and a big cattleman. He had a housekeeper at the station, along with other Aboriginal women working there. Jim Davey was a funny bloke, different from Tommy Singer. He's the only man that I ever saw driving a Land Rover with spurs. I never worked out what they were for. Maybe he thought they would make the Land Rover go faster, or maybe he was just saving time when he got to the stock camp. I don't know which way he was thinking, but that's what he used to do. And he had one funny eye. He would have his hat down low, and when he'd turn his head to look at us, he used to screw up this one eye. Some fellas said that they knew he was just telling them a yarn when he did that.

That Land Rover wasn't the only car he drove around. We'd always see him with this other one. A long time after I left Granite Downs a white friend of mine told me it was a Bentley. And I don't know if it's true, but he told me this story. He reckoned that one time Jim Davey went down to Adelaide with a mob of cattle and when he's there he went to one of those motor-car places selling new Chryslers. The salesman saw him looking around, and Jim Davey's not very clean. Looking like a real bushy. Just wearing boots, pants on all right, but he'd be wearing this dirty blue singlet he'd always have on. So the salesman comes up to him, and Jim Davey asks him: "G'day. How much is this?" And the salesman says, "Well, now, it's too much for you, sir." So Jim Davey just said, "Oh", and went away. He went to another caryard then and bought this new Bentley. Drove it around to the first place, and waited outside in his car. When that same bloke comes over to him, Jim Davey said, "Oh, ah, fill 'im up, please."

At Granite Downs he always called us blackfellas. We didn't have a name, to him we were just blackfellas. He used to throw a bridle at me and say, "Hey, little blackfella, catch me camp horse." And when he talked to us, Jim Davey and some other whitefellas would use this different English, well, different from when they talked to each other. He'd say: "'im bin go thataway" or "You bin see 'im longadat horse?" or "You like 'im dat one?" So I thought that must be the proper way, and I was trying to talk like that. I'd say, "Oh, yeah, I like 'im dat one." We wouldn't use it when we talked to each other, we'd just use Yankunytjatjara. But the whitefella talked to us like that, and we learned it.

Oh, I was frightened of him, but it wasn't like that for every-body. If he got into an argument with the men, those *wati*, they'd pull out. I've seen it. Or they'd have a dust-up. They'd always be fighting over something to do with work – whitefellas and blackfellas. One time there was the biggest mob of cleanskins in the yard, ready for branding next morning, and Jim Davey did the wrong thing to one of those men. I think he picked the argu-ment, called him a blackfella or something. I don't know the full story. Anyway, that fella just pulled out and the others followed in sympathy. Yep, they all left him, and he couldn't do anything. He couldn't keep the cattle in the yard too long, so he had to open the gate and let them go. They'd just fix him like that.

One time I remember Hughie Cullinan was watching cattle. He was horse-tailer, so he'd taken the first watch that night, and he asked Jim Davey for tobacco: "Ah, *tjilpi*, any tabacca?" It was just a little thing, and Jim Davey said: "No, You don't want 'im tabacca. You got 'im pituri." You know, that bush tobacco, *mingkuḻ*. So Hughie told him: "All right, *tjilpi*, stick it up your arse. I'm pulling out in the morning." So Hughie went off, riding his night horse around the cattle. Jim Davey comes back and said to him: "Hiya, Hughie. Hiya. Look ah, here's tabacca." Hughie just told him to stick it up his arse again. And next morning he pulled out, he left the job. Ronnie Russell went with him. Hughie said to me: "Come on, you. Let's go." And I just stood there, never said anything. "*Tjitji awai!* I told you, come on. Let's go." But of course I didn't go with him, I stayed back with uncle Alec Baker. So they left their horses and walked to Lambina with just the clothes on their backs, their boots, and a bit of a swag.

They told me later that Jim Davey followed them in his Land Rover. When he found them, he said, "Come on, get inna car, I'll take you home." Hughie told him to get fucked, and they just kept walking. So Jim Davey met up with old Paddy Way at Alice Bore, near the New Lambina Homestead. He said to him: "Hughie Cullinan pulled out with Ronnie Russell this morning. When they get here, give 'im tabacca and all this. You can organise to shift the cattle from Bubalin Dam back to here." So he gave him tobacco, new shirts, trousers, and everything. When Hughie and Ronnie arrived, Paddy Way said: "Oh, look, I'm by myself here. I don't know what I'm going to do. Why don't you two men give me a hand?" And they did. So they went on working for Jim Davey anyway.

I suppose Jim Davey must've known that Anangu were the backbone of the cattle industry then, especially for him. He knew the dollars and cents part and the market, he can do that. He knew the bookkeeping. But blackfellas were doing the hard part. They were the industry when there were no fences.

He didn't really treat us badly at Granite Downs. Oh, they'd get wild with us if we were a bit rough with the horses. Say to us, "Look, go easy on the horse" or something like that. And we didn't get paid much. Oh, he'd feed us workers and he dressed us well all right. But the only time we got money was at Oodnadatta after trucking time, or during racetime – he had some good racehorses. Of course, a married man would get rations for his wife and kids. The government was feeding us, giving us blankets and all that. But it wasn't like stories I heard about other stations where they'd make Aboriginal men have a fight, boxing, before breakfast. And, I heard, give them a flogging, tie them up to a tree and give them a hiding with a whip. When I was working at Granite Downs, I never saw it like that. They'd just argue and sometimes they'd walk out. Jim Davey would have an argument with just about everybody, even his own nephew, Tommy Singer. I seen them just about to fight, but the uncle got in his car and took off back to the station. I think the whitefellas used to call him Old Ironbark. Now, I'm not sure how he got that name, but some people say he earned it because he was tough.

One other thing I knew about Jim Davey when I was there. He had a feeling for Hughie Cullinan. Hughie did a lot of good work for him, of course. And every time they'd truck cattle down to Gepps Cross market in Adelaide, he'd send Hughie Cullinan on the train as the drover, making sure that no cattle were lying down. Hughie reckons – he told me this years later – that when he got down south to Quorn the first time he went, there was a whitefella waiting at the station, probably the stock agent. And he kept on asking if Hughie Davey was there. It took Hughie a while to work out that it was him that fella was looking for. I think Jim Davey just about wanted Hughie to be his son. He'd always look after him, give him just about everything Hughie asked for, you know, good things for stock work, like that. I don't think he had a son of his own.

He's finished now, Jim Davey. He owned the Aileron pub later on, and they told me that one night when he was working he died behind the bar. It was a sad way to go.

Anyway, I remember once, it was during hot time, all the *wati* knocked off, had a holiday. When I was at Granite Downs, we didn't work all year. We'd start about March and go until the end of November. They gave me a spell too, but I stayed on with those whitefellas. Mostly I'd be with Tommy Singer. I went everywhere on Granite Downs with him. He once shot a big wild stallion, and I watched him look at the teeth to tell how old he was. And he'd cut off the tail and the mane.

Around the station he'd teach me other things. He showed me how to stretch the bullock hide on an old iron buggy wheel, then put salt on it and leave it out to dry. And when they dropped a killer, he used to get all the fat from the guts and kidneys and reduce it down outside in two buckets: one with onion and a little bit of kerosene, and later mix the other one with Stockholm tar. He'd take that first bucket and keep on pressing the fat to get the oil, until it was clear. When we were breaking in horses or when we went mustering, we used to take those two buckets, might be more. But anyway two: one with tar and the other one's clear. With the bullock hides, he'd wet the ground and bury them in the mud for maybe a day. Then, he'd take them out and cut the hide into strips. He'd make hobble straps then, and head ropes and leg ropes. I wasn't very good at it, but I saw them do it. Putting what they call a Turk's head, like plaiting it, I suppose. Then he'd start me up and show me how to grease them with that clear fat to make them soft. But not too soft, or the horse would stretch it out and it'd come undone. The one with the Stockholm tar, he showed me how to put it on a horse's sore back or around the girth. A young horse, just learning to walk with hobbles, would cut himself around the fetlock. Sometimes they'd be badly cut, especially when they were a bit wild, hopping around with the hobbles, and we couldn't catch them. So he'd teach me to put it around there.

Then we started shifting cattle, because water was getting low in the dams and in the waterholes. And we'd go out and make sure the bores and windmills were working properly. At some bores there'd be a small camp — just one old fella and maybe his wife — and they'd start the pump-jack in the morning and go out for kangaroo the rest of the day. They'd call them *intjina tjapata*. Tommy Singer'd be showing me how to fix the bores: the right way to put on the chain tong and Stillsons and which way to unscrew the pipe, how to replace the pump buckets. He was pulling the bores with his Land Rover. He'd be working, whistling that favourite song of his, and then say to me, "This is how you do it Wallatina Kid."

I remember one time, a lot of the men were back from out bush. We had the biggest mob of horses in the drafting yard, getting ready to put the camp out. One young bloke had this sleeveless jumper he used to wear, might've been a footy jumper, with a big number thirteen on the back. But all the men — Whisky and the rest of them — reckoned that he was a flash rider, number thirteen rating on the rodeo circuit. I told them he played football and that was his number. That's just what they put on their jumpers. But they wouldn't believe me: "No, no. That's what rodeo riders wear. Does he think he can beat this horse?" They went over to Rex and asked him if he wanted a go.

So they drafted in this mare, a black and white piebald mare. Pretty looking. She had a foal and they drafted that out into another yard. I said to this young fella, "Hey, friend, horse no good." I think he understood me, but he wouldn't listen, he wanted to ride. I reckon he didn't want to be a coward in front of other ringers. They put a bridle and saddle on her and Whisky said to him: "Don't frighten her with the saddle on. You just get up there." Poor thing, they nearly killed that lad. And I

60

was ashamed. But he had a lot of guts to try, I'll give him that. When he was laying on the ground, I could see Whisky and the others laughing: "Hahaha. He'll never wear that number thirteen again."

I was with Hughie Cullinan a lot that time. He was good with the young teenagers, boys like Wallace and Ginger and Andrew Breaden. But not with me. I don't know, but to him I was a naughty boy, I think. And he just couldn't stop himself doing something to me all the time. One time we were both horse-tailers, out at Ninety-nine Waterhole, shoeing horses. Some of the horses were wild buggers, they wouldn't let us shoe them, so we had to throw them down. Then Hughie'd say, "Righto, righto. Hold 'im down, hold 'im down!" And I'd be struggling: "No, no brother, I'm worryin' 'bout his head." And he'd say, "*Tjitji awai!* Don't give me that. Hold 'im!" So I'd be hanging on to the bridle and he'd put a collar rope around their neck. And from that double rope, he'd tie a leg rope down the side, hook it around the fetlock and pull tight. The horse didn't like it, of course, so he'd kick and fart and want to fight.

One horse was real touchy, we couldn't even pick his feet up. So we threw him down, tied him up, and Hughie just sat down holding the horse's head. Then I'd have to shoe all four hooves while Hughie's rolling cigarette after cigarette. "Come on, quick, I can't be sittin' here holding his head all the time. I gotta lot to do." And I'd be there going flat out, and he'd be saying, "Quick, quick, quick! Come on, drive the nail. Right. Now, break 'im off! Bend it now!" We'd do quite a few of them like that. When the others came back from mustering, we knocked off for dinner too. And Hughie'd be sitting down eating and say to them: "Aah, *wiya*. Nope, that kid is just lazy. This is one lazy bugger. I've been shoein' horses by myself all day." He'd turn to Ronnie Russell and give him a nudge: "And *wati*, I shoe your horse too. Just me. And that kid did nothing." And I just sat there and took it. I couldn't do anything else: I was a kid, and he was a man, you know. I think he did it just to see what I'd say, but I just sat back and smiled.

We'd then go to a place called Iliyampa Waterhole, a big

waterhole at the Todmorden boundary. Me and Hughie again. And there was this big chestnut horse, big white blaze from his forehead to the nose and four white socks. Pretty, but cunning as a fox. We called him *papa inura*. So I said to Hughie, "Oh, I gotta ride that bastard." And he said: "Oh, now, you can just wait. We'll be a long time catching that one. He's cunnin', you know." But I wanted to ride him. "No, come on. Rope him for me." So he did, choked him almost. I put the bridle on, he gave me a hand to saddle him, and held it for me while I got on. And he just bucked like anything. I was just sitting loose, swinging my legs, and hanging on.

We followed up the creek to Fox Hole with a mob of horses, and this horse I was on was bucking all the way. Hughie said to me, "Hey, gallop up front. Make 'im gallop 'long the creek. That'll bugger 'im up." So, I really sweat him up then. When we arrived at the dinner camp, Hughie told me to gallop up and block the front of the mob of horses. So I kicked mine to go forward. Oh, no. He just dropped his block and give it me. I managed to stay on again and rounded up the other horses. When we were having dinner with the others, I could see Jimmy Wallatina wasn't happy: "Oh, I just don't like that horse of mine. He's always giving me a sore stomach." So I said to him, "Give it to me. Come on, bros, give it to me. I'll knock 'im up." So he did. I'd just played with that horse all day!

I think Tommy Singer must've seen I was doing all right, because next time they walked fat cattle to the railhead at Oodnadatta, he told me I was going too. I don't think I'll ever forget it. Allan Downs was with us, and Ginger Mofila. And there were a lot of whitefellas: Tommy Singer, of course, and Tommy Kempster – I got to know him real well after that – and an old whitefella with long whiskers, his name was Eli Johnson. All experienced men, you know. And there were some other young fellas. The cattle were good that time and I don't really know – I wasn't very good at how many days there were in a week, or months and years then – but I think it took us maybe three weeks to get there. They didn't want to flog them, so they would lose condition, so we went slow, maybe six miles a day.

When we got to Oodnadatta, we camped near a little sandhill just east of the town.

It wasn't always that way. It wasn't always as easy walking cattle to the railhead. Once, later on, we were taking thirteen hundred head – I remember that number because that's what the manager, said. There were two whitefellas, five men and one kid – that's me. I was on first watch, and it was good that night. It was cold, but clear, and the cattle were quiet. I was supposed to watch them from seven until nine o'clock. I couldn't tell the time, but I remember that's what Hughie told me. I was riding this beautiful night horse. We only rode them at night, and they were wonderful. Sometimes a steer might wander away and we might not see it, but those night horses just knew. They'd turn, and we'd slacken the reins and let him have his head, and he'd just go around and pick it up, bring him back to the mob.

The second night was different. Hughie had taken over from me, and I was asleep in the swag. I don't know how long I was there when I woke up and heard this noise. I could see everybody was running for cover, so I ran to a tree too. The cattle were stampeding. I'd never seen it before, and somebody said: "That's it, they've started now. They'll be doing it all the way to Oodna." Alec Baker and Treacle were off chasing them and the two whitefellas jumped on the other night horses. The other men were grabbing their bridles and going out to the hobbled horses. When I finally came out from the tree, I was the only one left behind.

Uncle Alec told me that when they stampede like that, to gallop on the side and try to reach the lead ones. But not to block them or they'll just run over us. We had to spin the lead around so they would come back towards the tail. They'd gallop around a bit, then stop, pick their heads up, and sort of walk around going "mmmmmmmmmrrrrrrahhhhhhhh". They'd all have a piss then. And we kept talking to them to get them quiet.

He nearly got killed that night, my uncle. They told me later he was wheeling the cattle around when his horse stumbled and fell in a rabbit burrow. The cattle were almost on him, and he jumped up yelling "*Paiyai!*" and throwing sand in the air. The

63

mob of bullocks just split around him, with my uncle in the middle with his horse. That night he was lucky, but we lost a hundred head to unknown country. I thought they were joking when they said the cattle'd be stampeding every night until we got to Oodnadatta. But they did.

Anyway, that first time we went to Oodnadatta, about the only thing I knew about the place was that it was where they took the cattle for trucking on the train to Adelaide. I thought it was a big town. Some Anangu were living there, some Yankunytjatjara and Southern Arrernte from Macumba. Near the railway line was the mission. There were quite a few houses. People called Green lived there, and the station-owners had houses too, where they'd stop when they were in town trucking cattle or going to the races. People working for the railway lived there too. And I'd never even seen a train before that. The first time I saw one, coming along the track, I thought it was a lot of little houses moving along the ground. I just couldn't work out what it was.

Me and Ginger were tailing cattle. And all those big people who were with us never came to give us a hand. So we were watching them, and the sun was getting low. We'd bring the mob close to the camp and settle them down for the night. We'd ride around on a night horse and sing *inma*: "Davey, Davey Crockett…" Something like that. Tommy Singer's favourite song when he rode around the cattle was "Irene, goodnight". Took me a long time to work out if that was his horse's name, the cattle's name, or what.

We were still on our day horses when we got the cattle closer to the camp, but nobody'd got the night horses ready. So we settled the cattle down. We could see the whitefellas drinking. Grogging on. Just laughing, swearing at each other, not seriously, but they'd say, "Aaah, get faahked, ya baahstard." They were just having a good time. So we're riding around and around the cattle, and I said to Ginger, "*Tjuu*, you keep goin' 'round and I'll go and find Tommy Kempster and that old man, Allan Downs." Tommy Kempster was the horse-tailer, so I went over to him and said, "Hey, *tjilpi*, wake up. *Wai, nyanytju wai?*

Where's the night horses? You gotta go on first watch." And he was just going "uughaaa". I think rum kicked him in the head. Allan Downs was in his swag and he was no better.

So I got on my horse, and I can see the other fellas. Two of them are in their swags, finished. The other two are sitting and drinking, not taking any notice of what we're doing. They were off their faces. They had sort of a grog face, you know? That old fella, Eli Johnson, was trying to cook, and I was worrying about his long white whiskers catching alight. So I went back to Ginger and said, "*Tjuu*. They're all drunk. I'll go and get four night horses. Then I'll have a cuppa tea." I went and got the horses, led them back and tied them to a tree, and put on a nose-bag with lucerne chaff. So they're standing there eating, that's their job. Then I had a quick feed. I didn't even bother to go to our camp, I just ate it right there in front of that old whitefella.

Then I saddled up for the first watch. I said to Ginger: "Righto, *tjuu*. You can have your tea, then have a sleep. Looks like it's gonna be a long night for me and you, 'cause it looks like the rest of 'em are finished." So he goes off. I start riding around, singing some rubbish song so the cattle get used to the noise. They were good, very quiet, just lying there sleeping. Then more whitefellas turn up in a car and unload some people and go back. They were ringers from Granite Downs, with more grog. They're all real happy, standing by the fire with their arms over another bloke's shoulders, singing: "Davey, Davey Crockett. King of the wild frontier..." And they're all together going forward to the fire and back.

Then they throw this young, short fella right in. I was riding around, watching this, and I thought, "Now, should I leave 'im there to burn, or do I go and pull 'im out? No, I'm looking after cattle. It's their faahkin' cattle, not mine." Then that short bloke starts crying out: "*Waiiii*, ya faahkin' baahstards." The others didn't take any notice of him. They just went back drinking. So I gallop up, propped the horse right close to the fire, and jumped off at the same time. I dragged him away, and I could see he was burned on both legs. He was crying, and I thought, "Yeah, well. You dumb prick."

Ginger woke up and I said to him: "*Tjuu*. You'll have to look after the cattle. Looks like I'll have to take this fella into town." I saddled up the other night horse, and tried to put him on. So I'm leading his horse into town and he's bent forward in the saddle, crying. It was dark, and I didn't know where I was going. My eyes weren't the best anyway. I might not have mentioned it before, but I had only one eye and it wasn't very good. Something happened to the other one when I was at Wallatina. I got over the railway line all right and kept going. Then the horse stopped. I took my foot out of the stirrup and started to feel around. Oh, it's a fence. It's the fence around the airstrip. I knew I should've asked Ginger to go – he's been in Oodnadatta before. So I turn the horse around and find my way to sort of a street with houses on the left and right. And I came to a place with lights on inside and people talking. I know what that place is now: it's the Oodnadatta pub. There's a hitching rail in front, so I tied up my horse. That young fella couldn't get down from the saddle and he's crying. I just left him there.

I went to the door and knocked. A white woman opened it, and a whitefella came out too. She said, "Yes?" I pointed to where the horses were. He was still crying and calling out, "Haaalp, haaalp." They raced out and took him inside. Never said anything to me. So I waited, standing around with my two horses. I was thinking, "Now, what I gotta do? Where do I go?" Car comes up, a big V8. It's the Oodnadatta police sergeant. I found out later his name was Bruce Evans. He says, "Where's the camp?" So I pointed to the sandhill. And off he goes.

And I'm still waiting. After a while I think, "Well, I suppose they're finished with me, so I'll go." When I got back to the camp Ginger was still going around and around the cattle. He told me that the police had come and talked to the fellas. I went over to Allan Downs and tried to wake him up, but I couldn't. It was the middle of the night by now, and I said to Ginger: "*Wai, tjuu*. What do we do?" "You have a sleep," he told me. "I'm pretty right. I'll wake you up in a while." So I went to sleep. When Ginger got tired, I took over the watch. We did that all night.

About five o'clock in the morning, Tommy Singer woke up and came over to me: "Oh, allrightnowallright. You go sleep. I'll take over now." He looked a little sober, and when I got to my swag I could hear him singing: "Irene, goodnight, Irene…" Just before sunrise, he made the cattle get up, let them walk around and have a feed. I think Tommy Kempster sort of woke up then. He must've remembered he was supposed to be the horse-tailer, so he went and got some horses. Me and Ginger were still in the swag, but we got up anyway. We had enough sleep. We were young, you know, full of life and didn't want to sleep all day.

We let the cattle feed all next day, and the day after that we took them to the trucking yard and drafted them out in separate yards according to size. Then the big cattle station owner, Jim Davey, turns up. He talked to the fellas at the sandhill camp first. Then he came over to see me and Ginger at the trucking yard, waiting for the train. He sits between us on the top rail of the yard, and pats us on the back. He's smiling at us and saying something in that way of his. He talked through his teeth somehow, so he'd whistle at the end of his words. I could see he was happy anyway. And we thought we were in trouble.

After we got the cattle on the train, he sacked four or five of those whitefellas. I suppose he paid them off. Then he asked me and Ginger to go to old Jack Hanney's with him. He was an ex-police sergeant and he had a shop and he ran the Royal Post. Jim Davey just bought everything for us, dressed us up from toe to top: R. M. Williams boots, gaberdine, and light smokey blue shirt. Bahh! Proper deadly. And he even gave us cash. We were the best-looking ringers in the place, with all these two bobs jingling in our pockets. When we got out of Jack Hanney's, Ginger said, "Tonight, *tjuu*, we don't have to worry about bullocks. We'll just hobble the horses out and go to the picture show."

Well. I'd never seen a picture show, and that night when I did, I thought it was fair dinkum, you know, the real McCoy. One interesting thing was that all the whitefellas were inside a sheet-of-iron building watching the movie, and all the blackfellas were outside looking through the windows. That's one thing I noticed. So, if those were the rules it must be right. I don't know. I was still a bush kid, but I reckon it might've been if you pay, you go inside; if you don't pay, you can watch through the windows. I didn't pay. Lucky they had enough windows. I remember it was a cowboy picture.

And I seen that young fella, the one that got burnt, and he didn't get the boot from Jim Davey. He came around and he wanted to talk, but I couldn't understand him. Those other fellas caught a train going north. One bloke, young fella by the name of Johnny Long, he tried to take us with him. He said to me and Ginger, "Come on, you blokes, come with us. We'll go to Mt Dare. We'll run amuck." But we said no. They climbed up the Ghan, saying goodbye to everybody, and off they went. Gee, I wish I could meet those fellas now, I'd like to have a yarn. I just couldn't communicate with them then, because of the language barrier.

It wasn't long after I got back to Granite Downs Station that I had a chance to go to my old home. We were breaking horses again. Alec Baker and Allan Downs were there, and me and Ginger. I don't know where Wallace was. Tommy Singer and Tommy Kempster were with us too, and two other young white-fellas. Then they said we were going to Wallatina. So we rode through Wantjapila, Mt John, Alpanyinta, and I remember we stopped at Larry Well, Tjinawakanytja.

There was a stockyard at Larry Well with a trap gate; when a horse comes in for a drink, it can open the gate but it can't get out again. We set the trap gate for the night and came back next morning; we'd got us some brumbies. There were two that interested us: one was black all over, and the other one was fat and just beautiful-looking: big white blaze, and two white socks on the hind legs. Tommy Singer broke in that one, and Allan Downs was breaking in the other. They worked on them all day, and in the afternoon they were riding them around. Tommy Singer's horse had a good nature. The jet black one was just an outlaw. Allan was riding it, but I think it could've killed him.

We rode the new horses back to Wallatina. Mrs Cullinan was there, I hadn't seen her in years. Tjilpi Tommy Cullinan had passed away since I'd gone, so the Cullinans' son Bill had taken charge of the cattle work. *Tjamu* Dicky was still there, though, and so was my uncle Harry Wallatina. Mrs Cullinan brought us all morning tea and homemade cakes, the same kind of cakes she used to give me when I was a nanny-goat shepherd.

Tommy Singer wanted us to go back to old Marla Bore, to Ernie Giles' stock camp, so after morning tea we set off, through Tjinawakanytja, travelling east. We teamed up with a party from Welbourne Hill and mustered for a few days around Rock Hill Well, east of Marla, then drafted out the Granite Downs cattle from the mob. From there we split up, they all went on to Welbourne Hill Station, and we turned back to Wantjapila along the old Stuart Highway. I remember this old whitefella and his missus, tourists I'd call them now, who saw us and started talking to us. They gave us oranges, then got the camera out. So we lined up, three blackfellas in our stockman outfits, and they took our photo.

Tommy Singer and the rest of them caught up with us at Wantjapila. Bill Cullinan started taking the cattle back to Wallatina, but Tommy Kempster said, "Ah, you and me are going to Welbourne Hill." So we headed south-east, and at Welbourne Hill homestead, I met up with my old grandfather, Secretary. He's a Welbourne Hill *wati*, an important man for that place. Me and Secretary had to take horses from Welbourne Hill to Wintinna, while Tommy Kempster and Ernie Giles went in the car.

We mustered around the Wintinna area for a while. I was doing a double job: in the morning I'd be horse-tailer and during the day I'd be tailing cattle with Tjilpi Secretary. Tommy Kempster was off with the other fellas mustering. All the time mustering. A steady rain set in, and kept up all night. That morning, before dawn, when I was out getting the horses for the camp, this big bay horse I was riding walked onto a rabbit warren. Horses usually see the burrows, but it couldn't have seen this one. The ground was so soft the warren caved in. His two front legs sunk down, and I went head first into a rabbit hole. He got up and stepped backwards, waiting for me. I got up with my hat sideways, covered in wet sand. I was laughing to myself, but I was lucky I didn't break any bones.

All day it rained. Me and Secretary were trying to make the cattle move forward: walking and walking and walking. My hands were that cold they were numb. The whitefellas were the same. We saw an old *kaṉku* by an old shepherd's camp and Secretary just sat down and lit a fire. Must've been the right thing to do, because all those whitefellas came around to get warm.

The ground became very soft from the rain. The cattle and the horses could hardly move in the thick mud. We had lunch over by the truck that was travelling with us, then we tried to make the cattle get up and go again. But the ground was just too boggy. Some whitefella said, "Oh, faahk 'em. Leave the baah-stards." So we did and went back to the road – the old Stuart Highway. Tjilpi Secretary was finished, his teeth were rattling. Poor thing. He was an old man. I was a young fella, but I was cold. Tjilpi Kempster went ahead with the horse-tailers. We were a bit behind, dragging the chain a bit, and this one white-fella, he was sort of good type of bloke, was waiting for us. I think he was a sort of a boss.

When we finally got to the camp the others had made, it was dark. I heard this German bloke, Fred Roosh, say to that white-fella we were with: "Yeah! The faahkin' baahstards! Leave the faahkin' cattle. Can't drive in this faahkin' rain." Then they had the biggest argument. I thought they were going to start fighting. Another one was saying: "Cut it out, you two. Come on, settle down." And I was trying to undo the saddle, but my hands were so cold I just couldn't feel a thing. Tommy Kempster came over and told me to go and get warm. He hobbled out my horse and hung the saddle on a tree. Benny Gibbs had made a lovely *kaṉku* for the three of us, and a little fire going. So we camped there that night, nice and warm. Next morning it was still raining, but the cloud was breaking up.

By the time we got to Welbourne Hill it had fined up, but we were just stuck there waiting for the ground to dry out. We couldn't get back to Granite Downs, so we left the horses in the

Welbourne Hill horse paddock. We sat down at the station in one of the sheds. It seemed to me we were there for a long time, waiting for it to dry up. Tommy Kempster used to do leather work, and he plaited a hatband and he made little leggings for me. On the leggings he made a pouch and put a pocket knife in it. Then he made a leather thing to hang on my belt for wax matches. And he gave me new, green gaberdine trousers and this lovely shirt. It was sort of off-white, and it had green cuffs, with one, two, three buttons. And there were rhinestones sewn into the material. It laced up the front and on each of two pockets was a bullock's head on the flaps. He gave me all those things, and I thought it was pretty good of him.

When it was dry enough, me and Tommy headed back to Granite Downs. I could see the biggest mob of stockmen when we got there: Treacle, Wangka, Whisky, Alec Baker, Hughie Cullinan. But I just didn't want to go over, I don't know, I just felt shy. So I started unpacking the packhorses, when Wangka and Hughie come over. Wangka says, "Hello, boy." Hughie looks me up and down and says, "Hey, *tjitji awai!* Poor thing, you're not a stranger. You know us!" Then he saw my shirt, the one Tommy Kempster gave me back at Welbourne Hill. "Hey, what's this? Come on, take that shirt off and give it to me now!" But I just stood there, never said anything. I had early supper outside the homestead and went off to the saddle shed where I used to sleep.

I was at the station for a while then, maybe a month. We were doing odd jobs. One evening, after we had our dinner, Hughie told me and Wallace to come with him to the main community for a visit. Whisky and Wangka came with us. So we all started walking, and Hughie was saying to me and Wallace, "Hey, don't sleep in tomorrow, you got to get the horses." He kept on saying the same thing, and I'm thinking: "Now, why's he saying that over and over? He knows that I can get up and get a horse, he knows that. I'm a horse-tailer. I know the job. I'm a ringer. Why is he telling me this? There's something going on here."

On the way to the main community was the *nyiinka* camp,

and we stopped and sat down with them. But I was feeling uncomfortable. Every time Hughie said anything, he had this little smile, which I didn't like. So I was thinking: "Oh, I don't know, I don't want to stop here too long. I might go back." My brother Wallace, he didn't seem to notice a thing. If he did, he didn't let on. So I got up, making out I was going to have a piss. I went around this prickly wattle bush and had a look at the main camp in the distance. Then I started thinking: "Right. I don't know what's going on, but I'm going to have to look after myself." That was all right, I was just *tjitji kungkatja*, a teenage kid. When I got there, I saw a big, long windbreak. Everybody was lying down. Then I recognised it: *irkapiri* camp. "Oh, hello," I'm thinking. "Now, what's going to happen?" I just stood there and looked, then nothing. Looked like everybody was just lying down, waiting for something to happen.

So I turned to go, and noticed one of our grandfathers sitting by a little fire and windbreak. Then I saw another one of the grandfathers walking around. "Come on, grandson," the first grandfather says. "Sit down by this fire." So I sat down. The *irkapiri* camp was behind me, and the way I was facing I could see Wallace back at the *nyiinka* camp and I was watching him. It was getting a bit dark and I couldn't see that far. But I wasn't happy: I like to know what's happening. So I'm sort of squatting, not properly sitting down, and my *tjamu* is saying to me, "Come on, sit down, grandson." Get your bum on the ground and cross your legs, he meant. So I said, "I'm fine, *tjamu*."

Then somebody tried to grab Wallace but he bolted, and the men started singing out, *"Pau, pau"*, and we guessed what they were up to. They were going to put us through, make us *nyiinka*. As soon as I heard that, I jumped up. My *tjamu* jumped up. He went for me, but he missed. I ran straight past the *irkapiri* camp for the fence line, with my two grandfathers right behind. I got under the fence, and saw cattle watering at the trough. I just went through them, but they pulled up my grandfathers because they didn't know much about what the cattle might do. I ran all the way back to the station, got my swag, and went to the saddle room. I was shaking, trying to catch my breath. I locked the door from the inside and threw my swag on top of some hay. Then I got in, and lay there catching my breath.

Next morning, I woke up early, got the bridle, and took off. I found the horses and counted them up. Yeah, there're enough here. I caught this big grey gelding, the one I usually ride bareback. Just as I was about to pull myself up, I heard this man's voice behind me, "Hey, block the horses." I looked up and it was my brother Hughie Cullinan. My sparring partner. He's standing there, and I shit myself. I'm sure I did. "Ah, no! What's he gonna do now? Have I made a mistake, or what?" He just quietly said to me again: "Block the horses. I wanna catch a ridin' horse."

We drove the mob of horses back and put them in the yard. I took the bridle off and carried it back to this long rail where the saddles are sitting. I went over to the fire where we used to have breakfast and dinner. There was the biggest mob of men there: Whisky and Wangka, all of them, and others too. I just grabbed my favourite quart pot (the one Tommy Singer gave to me), poured tea from the billy, grabbed the knife and cut the damper and salt beef, and went to sit down by myself under the rack with the bore columns and casings. I knew they were all watching me, and I thought: "I've got no friends now. I'm the only kid around here now."

I knew I hadn't done anything wrong the night before, really. When that *irkapiri* camp is going, and the men try to catch the boys or the *nyiinka*, you can get away. They never tell you what's going to happen, and they've got to trick you into it. So what I did wasn't unusual. I was just more clever than they were. At least I thought I was when they were watching me eating my breakfast that morning. I could see Hughie pouring a cup of tea, cutting damper, and looking at me with his funny smile. "You snake," I thought. I didn't like this. I know he's going to just keep on rubbishing me. He's going to give me a hard time, the snake. But the others, like all my uncles – Whisky and Wangka and Alec Baker – they were different towards me. And that's the way it is: your uncles are suppose to be like your friends. But brothers like Hughie...

73

So that's how it was when we went out that day to get bullocks around the station for killer and we did some branding as well. Hughie was really rubbing it into me. He made me work hard in the yard: roping calves, throwing them, holding their legs. And he'd just keep on saying, "You crummy kid. *Tjitji kungkatja. Kuya-kuya.* Just a kid." Like that. Wallace, my old friend, wasn't there. I suppose he was a *nyiinka* now, separate from the others. Then Hughie said, "Oh, we're going to see him soon, your friend Wallace."

I don't know how many days later, Wallace came back to work. I had to speak differently to him now, sort of sideways. I'd say: "Oh sorry. Ah, *wai?*" He'd ask if there were any cigarettes around, and I gave him tobacco from the pocket of my gaberdines. *Tjitji kungkatja* like me have to be frightened of *nyiinka*. You can't be cheeky to *nyiinka* because he's been with the men. They've spoken to him about things. If you get cheeky, if you swear at him or anything like that, he can give you a good hiding. My father had told me all these things before, at Wallatina. I knew the rules about how to behave to *nyiinka*, and to the men. So all right, *palya*.

We started on a big muster then, tender muster, south and south-east from the homestead. That country, Granite Downs, is the worst place for stock work. I suppose that's why they gave it that name. It goes well. The ground's rocky and uneven, and we were shoeing horses all the time. Just about every day the horses will throw a shoe. We mustered out from all the watering points around there: Magpie Waterhole, Christmas Well, Guts Ache Bore, Fox Hole, Ninety-nine Waterhole, Broken Leg Waterhole. Funny names they had. After that we drafted out all the cattle at Old Lambina.

Sometime after that, we went out to New Lambina Bore, east of Old Lambina, right on the Todmorden boundary. We were track riding. There was a wide creek there, they called it the Alberga, and we used to camp in it sometimes. Hughie Cullinan was there along with Wallace Wallatina and two young teenagers: me and Ginger Mofila. And Tommy Kempster. Jim Davey had come out to talk to him. We'd just gotten new clothes, new riding gear, Log Cabin tobacco, and wax matches, the ones with blue heads that we could light on anything. So we had all the nice things that he gave us.

Tommy Kempster was the cook. Some cooks weren't much for Anangu. They'll just give us two pieces of damper: one with salt beef on it, the other one with golden syrup. And tea. If we were still hungry we could go back and get another piece of damper and jam. Of course, whitefellas who are working get their proper tucker, you know, with vegetables and all that: potatoes and onions and carrots. We might have our own food sometimes, but not often. Treacle used to kill rabbits with stones, and Tommy Singer used to give us a rifle for kangaroo. But it wasn't like when we were living at Wallatina. When we were tailing cattle during the day we might see something and get off our horses and eat it, but the bosses didn't like it. If we lost the cattle or horses because we're too busy looking for *kampurara* or something, there was trouble for us. They'll give us a hiding if we lost them. This happened to me one time. Tommy Kempster was different; he would feed everyone the same. When I was a horse-tailer, I used to get firewood for him, and he used to get me to dig a long trench in the ground for all his different camp ovens, you know, bedouries. I think he had ten or more, with different things in them.

When other cooks had dinner or supper ready, they would cut the damper and give us some. One bloke would have this D-shaped billycan, and the cook would fill it from a big bucket. Not Tommy Kempster. He'd sing out: "Dinner's ready. Come on, I want six or seven blokes." We'd go over and he might have six or seven different trays of all these lovely different foods. Yep, so we used to have a good feed, and we used to like him as a man, and as a cook too.

But us Aboriginal people would still eat in our own camp. White people had their different place. That didn't worry us, that's how it was. Anyway, we had our own language, Yankunytjatjara, to talk; we didn't have to mix up English and Yankunytjatjara then. Those white people were over there, talking one language too, so that was all right.

Anyway, after Jim Davey finished talking to Tommy Kempster and went back to the station, Tommy came over and talked to Hughie and the rest of us. We didn't understand that language, except for Hughie. Well, I didn't. Hughie told us we had to go tender muster at Eringa Station – Kidman's big place. So we travelled to Pitjiri Bore and met up with all the stockmen from Eringa. We mustered all along the boundary with Granite Downs, right up to Dalhousie and Mt Dare. Then we came to the railhead at Abminga, and drafted out the ones that belonged to Granite Downs. There was a lot of people there too, from other stations just north, trucking their cattle: Andado, New Crown, Tieyon. And Eringa was trucking theirs. We had to walk with ours back to New Lambina.

After we got past Pitjiri Bore, the country is just sandhills, no water. There's one dry creekbed with big shady gum trees and we had to cross that. Tommy Kempster, Ginger, and me were driving the cattle. Wallace and Hughie had taken the packhorses. They caught up with us by the creek and gave us a drink of water. Tommy Kempster had a waterbag, carried around his horse's neck. So we had one waterbag between us. Before Hughie and Wallace left, they said, "We'll meet you back at New Lambina, at the boundary fence." Because we had cows and calves, we'd be travelling very slow.

I was new to that country. We're travelling and travelling, and there were sandhills stretching out to the horizon. Ginger and Tommy Kempster were on the wings and I was behind the mob. Then I noticed the sandhills were all facing east, and I started wondering: "Now, that's funny. There's something wrong here." I said to Ginger: "Hey, listen, bros. You know when we come from Lambina, goin' to Pitjiri Bore to meet up with those stockmen, we were crossing sandhills. This time those sandhills are lying in the same way. We're not going up and over, you know, and we should be. We should be going south." By this time, the cattle were getting tired, they just wouldn't move. I wanted to talk to Tommy Kempster, so we came around and he sort of stopped, saying, "Whassa matter?" He's rolling his cigarette. He loved his cigarette, that old man.

And I said to Ginger anyway, "Look. You stay with *tjilpi* and the cattle. I'm going back along our track to see where Hughie and Wallace went with the horses."

So I went back. Of course, I couldn't see a long way very well because my eyesight was so poor, but I could still pick up tracks. I could still tell the difference between horse and cattle tracks. When I got to where we turned off, I saw which way the others went. And then I knew we were going east, out into the scrub, instead of going south. I don't know why they turned the cattle that way, but we were going bush.

When I got to Ginger, I said, "We've taken the wrong turn. Now what we gonna do? How we gonna tell *tjilpi*? You got a little bit English?"

"Oh, yeah. I can tell him. I can say 'that way', you know."

"Well. I think you might sit with him. Leave the bullocks to me and have a rest. I'm OK for now." I could see the bullocks were tired.

Ginger went over to talk to Tommy Kempster. Later on, we decided to make the cattle get up and go back the way we came. I said to Ginger, "You ride in front so you can see the horse tracks and then we'll be right. We'll turn left then." Not very good English, but it sounds plain in Yankunytjatjara. But because we went out so far, by the time we picked up the track the sun was just going down. Our waterbags were empty. We followed the horse track until dark.

The cattle were just knocked up. They weren't going anywhere, but we made a camp and kept the horses saddled, just in case. I was asleep at the tail end. Ginger was on the wing and Tjilpi Kempster was at the front, sort of blocking them.

When the sun came up, I went around to Tommy Kempster. I saw his horse still had the saddle and bridle on, just walking around and eating, but I couldn't find him! So I sang out, "Tjilpi!" I'm sure he can understand Yankunytjatjara, we talked to him enough. There he was, and he said, "Oh, we starting again?" So I said to Ginger: "You go up front, *tjuu*. Pick up the track, and we'll follow you."

I was moving the slow mob, *tjilpi* was on the wing, and we're trying to keep them in a line, not spread out. Just as we start off, I hear this noise to one side. And it wasn't a bullock. They go "Uuum" or "uuummmmeerrrh". And it wasn't a calf either. So what is this going "berrrrhhh"? I went a little bit to the right. I could still hear this noise, but I couldn't see it properly. Then my horse stopped. "Come on," I said. "Chkkchkkchkk." But he wasn't going any farther. Whatever it was, it was under a shady tree. Then I could see it: out comes a little baby camel! *Ngana*, little one!

I called out to Ginger: "Hey! Hey! *Tjuu! Tjuu!* Look at this."

He comes over. "Yeah. Oh, very nice. Well, look out for the father and the mother. They'll get wild with you."

"Oh, shit!"

But they weren't around. And then the little one started following the cattle. Thought it was his mob. We kept going. Ginger was still up front, and I was still hunting the ones behind. Tjilpi Kempster was just walking, and all we could think about was water and food. Then we heard galloping. Wallace and Hughie. Coming back with the waterbags. And Hughie was wild with me. Typical.

"Ah, you useless baahstard, Yami!"

Then he turned to Ginger, but he was good to him: "What's wrong with you?"

"Oh, no, brother. We took the wrong turn."

Then back to me: "*Ai!* You're just a useless, rotten kid. Faahkin' bastard."

Then he gave us the waterbag and told us not to drink too much. So I drank just a little bit, then I took a mouthful. I started feeling funny in the tummy and I didn't know if I was going to vomit or what. Hughie must've been watching me: "I told you to take it slow, bloody kid."

The camp wasn't too far. Hughie rode up and talked to Tommy Kempster. The three of us just left the cattle then. Hughie and Wallace brought them in. When we got to the camp and unsaddled our horses, Tommy said, "Oh, don't hobble them up. Just let 'em go like it is." We had a drink of hot, black tea and ate some breakfast. Then the cattle arrived. They could just smell that bore water. They'd all string up along the fence line for a drink, and we just sat down.

But there was still work to do. Next day, we branded the young cleanskin calves. When we finished that, we just let 'em go. Opened the gate and let 'em go. Good. Now we can have a rest.

Car comes up, a Land Rover. It's Jim Davey. And he's got more new clothes. He squints at us and says, "Big mob, camp at Lambina. You gotta go." People from all the stations were there: Welbourne Hill, Everard Park, Kenmore Park, Tieyon, De Rose Hill, Todmorden. It was a big camp, all right. Cattle everywhere. Too many for the yard. When we finished cutting out, and they picked up their cattle and walked them back to their stations, Jim Davey wanted us to go to Hamilton and through to Macumba, both Kidman places.

I didn't know it then, but it was going to be my last trip as a stockman.

wati tawaritja – a young man

ngatun – prickly wattle

walytja tjuta – relations

intjina tjapata – engine shepherds

papa inura – wild dog

pau – exclamation to attract attention

irkapiri – close relatives of a *nyiinka*, a boy in ceremony stage

An eye for nothing

Hughie Cullinan and Tommy Kempster drafted out the horses at New Lambina yard for our trip to Hamilton. We got five riding horses each, and there were two camp horses, four night horses, and quite a few packhorses. Treacle had broken in this black stallion, and I was given that one to ride. I took a look at him and said to Hughie, "Ah, brother, I don't think I can ride this one. I don't like him, you know. And, anyway, I've got these sores, you know." I wasn't feeling the best. I had boils over the top of my legs and on my backside too. They were full of pus, and they hurt. I could see Hughie wanted to get going.

"Now what is it now, you bloody kid? Come on, let's go."

"*Wi… wiya*, no brother. I… I can't. He'll throw me. I can't."

Hughie just looked at me in that way of his, but he didn't push me hard. We started off east to Todmorden. I was riding this quiet piebald mare. The stallion came with us in the plant, but he was knocked out before we got to the station. He just stopped and wouldn't move. Tommy Kempster came over to me and smiled: "Oh, leave 'im. Just cut the neck strap and leave 'im there. I think his *ngampu* might be too big for 'im." Making a joke.

We stopped at the station that night, and next day went into country I didn't know. Late in the afternoon we arrived at Hamilton. The homestead was standing near some sandhills, and I could see a yard and windmill. Rusty Coombs was Kidman's manager. He had the biggest stockwhip I ever seen. They said it was twelve feet long, and he could handle it. He could make that whip go off like dynamite.

A whitefella by the name of Ray Wiley was there working as the cook. We went over to the Anangu camp where Tjilpi Dick Tjampita and some workers from Macumba were living. They were southern Arrernte people, but they could talk to us in Yankunytjatjara. I met two part-Aboriginal kids about my age. I could see they were mad like me by the way they played around with horses.

They had beautiful horses at Hamilton. Next morning they drafted them out, and we all started mustering at the different bores and waterholes. Plenty of water in that big-creek country. We mustered down the Alberga River and came to a place they called Number Ten Bore. The water just came out of the ground there, I think it must've been an artesian spring.

It was really hot, with an evil north wind blowing, and I was feeling worse and worse. My eyes were watering all the time, and I kept on rubbing them because they were sore. I was tailing cattle with this old Arrernte fella. He's finished now, poor bugger. The others had a big campdraft going, cutting out cattle and doing some branding.

Somebody said we had to leave because the yard wasn't big enough for all the cattle. That night we brought the cattle close to the camp and settled them down. When I finished, I just unsaddled my horse, hobbled him out, and got straight into my swag. I was sick now, really sick. I just lay there, trying to sleep, but I was hot and I had a headache. The others were all busy working, and I think they didn't notice me.

I can remember that night at Number Ten Bore clearly. The boss was talking about who was going to be on watch, and I was to go with that Arrernte fella and another bloke. But, later on, when they came to wake me up, I was almost too sick to get out of the swag. I got up, but when I opened my eyes I couldn't see properly. The same thing happened to me once before at Wallatina, when I was sick in both eyes, and later went blind in my right one. That night at Number Ten Bore, it was like opening my one good eye under water. I went over to where I thought the night horse was standing and tried to put the bridle on, but I was at the wrong end of the horse. I was lucky it didn't kick me. When I worked out which end was the head, I put the bridle and saddle on, but I wasn't sitting in the saddle properly. My legs were OK, but I was leaning over because of the pain in my head and in my eye. I was so hot. That Arrernte fella noticed me then, and asked me if I was sick. He told me to go lie down and don't bother about the cattle.

When everybody woke up early in the morning I was still in the swag. They were asking me what was wrong, and I was trying to open my eyes, but I couldn't see. I was blind. I put my hand in front of my face and I couldn't see it. I couldn't keep my eyes open for long because they were too sore. They left me there, and got busy, you know, doing the usual things. Grabbing their horses, packing them, and they're gone. I was still lying in my swag wondering if they were going to leave me there to die. The cook, Dick Tjampita, helped me get up and roll my swag and put it on the wagon. I just got in the back, kept my eyes shut, and lay there.

Later on they told me we were at the dinner camp, near a waterhole. I hadn't eaten dinner the night before or breakfast that morning, and I was vomiting. The manager from Macumba, John Kempe, arrived. I'm glad he did, for when he saw me he was more concerned than people in the camp. He came over and asked me what was wrong and then talked to the others. I think Hughie said to me, "He's gonna take you into Oodnadatta." I'm really grateful to that man, John Kempe.

So he took me to Macumba Homestead and organised for an Arrernte man to look after me. I don't know what his name was, but he was a lovely man. He was with me that night – gave me tea and meat. Next morning, John Kempe took me to Oodnadatta. I don't know how many days I was in the little clinic at the Australian Inland Mission, but it seemed like a long time. They were waiting to put me on the Ghan. The sister gave me tablets and eye drops. My eye was coming good by then. I could see a little bit, but everything was blurry. The kids from the United Aboriginal Mission used to come and visit me. They'd sit down and talk, and then they'd go home.

Then I think the mission sent word around saying they needed someone to take this boy down to Port Augusta on the train. They found Leslie Lester, another brother of mine. Poor thing, he's finished now. I remember quite a few people got on the Ghan with us. When me and Leslie got to Port Augusta, he got a taxi and we went to Umewarra Mission, just out of the town. It was my first taxi ride. Later that day we went to see the doctor.

His name was Dr Thompson, Dr J. R. Thompson. By this time I could see, but not a long way. I could see his room, the colour of the chairs, and what was on the walls. But I couldn't communicate. Leslie was my interpreter. The doctor asked all the questions.

"What's your name?"

"Yaminya."

And Leslie said, "Yaminya."

"What's your other name."

My other name? At that time Aboriginal people used to be shy about that. They weren't proud of using their own name with white people. I think I might have said before that mine came from one of my grandfathers, Tjiripingka.

"Oh, they call me Wallatina Kid."

I could see he didn't like that. And Leslie could see he didn't like it either.

So Leslie said, "Oh, um. Jim. They say Jim."

Now, Mr and Mrs Cullinan used to call me Jim sometimes at Wallatina. But it wasn't used much. I just used to go with Yami or, when I worked at Granite Downs, Wallatina Kid.

"All right. What about your last name?"

Leslie interpreted. I could see he wanted another name.

So Leslie said, "Lester. Jim Lester."

My new name.

After Dr Thompson looked at my eyes, they admitted me to the hospital. There was an Aboriginal man from Macumba in the same room. I remember he was showing me something through the window, but I told him I couldn't see what it was. Then I think it was the next morning when Leslie came and took me to the kitchen area for breakfast. My first whitefella breakfast, with plates and knives and forks, and I just couldn't handle it. So I used my hands. Dumb kid. Leslie looks at me and says: "No, no. Use your knife. Hey, that whitefella's looking at you." I told him to just forget the whitefella, and kept eating.

Then Leslie said they were taking me to Adelaide: "They can't fix you up here, so a white woman's going to take you." I don't know if the doctor told Leslie what was wrong with me, but if he did Leslie didn't tell me what he said. So this white woman, elderly lady with white hair, took me all the way to Adelaide. And from the railway station I could see all the high buildings, coloured ones and different ones. I became really interested. They were just like the Everard Ranges, only there was no open country. The woman took me in the taxi to the hospital. A doctor saw me there. Then they put me in a room with eight other beds. This is where all the fun started.

Oh, the nurses! They were beautiful. I watched their faces and looked at their different-coloured hair and, gee, they were beautiful women. I didn't know anything, of course. And this one lovely nurse – lovely she was, nice little round face, black hair with this little funny hat on top, and she's wearing a white apron – came in to see me, and I think she said, "What would you like for tea?" I couldn't really understand her, but I knew what tea was. So I said. "Oh, sugar." She laughed and said, "No, no. What you like for TEA?" I didn't know she was meaning supper, so I thought, "Now, what am I going to say? Next time she asks me I think I'll say milk." I can use the word milk. But in a funny way I suppose. I didn't really say MILK.

There was another fella in the room who was blind. I found out much later that he was a prospector by the name of Ron Kernick. He'd been out bush, Marree and Coober Pedy way. When the nurse finally gave up on me and left, somebody must've asked him if he could communicate with me. He said from his bed: "Oh, you bin supper, you know, you wannum supper, aaah, meat, ahhhh, meat, and bread?"

"Oh, *muntawa* – right. Ah yeah, me like 'im, yeah, me like 'im meat, um, me like 'im tomato." So Ron Kernick was sort of my other interpreter. And they gave me fritz and tomato and lettuce and all that stuff. It was all right; well, I mean I ate it anyway. Then I found out you can't go to the toilet. They gave me this little bottle: "You gotta use this." I think they said "water" or "wee-wee" or something. They were very nice, very nice girls. So that blind fella across the room sings out, "YOU GOTTA PISS IN IT." "Oh, yeah," I said, "I got 'im."

And when I wanted to go for the other job, the nurse showed me how to ring a bell beside the bed. So I'd do that, and the nurse came, and I'd say, "Me want 'im shit."

Her face changed then and she said, "I beg your pardon?"

And old Ron Kernick goes: "You can't go to the toilet. They bring 'im something for you. Shit 'im longa bed."

"Oh, me shit 'im longa bed? Me don't like dat one."

Anyway, to cut the long story short, I started moving around after a couple of days. This very nice nurse took me to the bathroom and showed me the bath. She looked beautiful. She put water in the bath, soap and face washer was there. I'm looking at her and thinking, "Gee, now what've I gotta do?" She told me I had to wash myself. I was a little bit shy, but I got in and was sort of hanging on to the side of the bath. I was just sitting there, so she showed me how to put water and soap on the face washer, and I said, "Oh, *muntawa*. Right, I got the idea." So I washed myself, got dressed, and I was feeling pretty good. But when I went back to the room the lights were off, and I found myself trying to get in somebody else's bed.

I don't know how long I was at the hospital, maybe seven or eight days. Ron's family – his wife and two kids – used to come and visit him. And this other old fella in the room would want to talk to me all the time in proper English, so Ron would translate in the language I can understand. The doctors and nurses didn't do anything to my eyes – no operation. They just would look at them with this little torch, then wash them with this funny-shaped dish and put in eye drops and ointment. Then I suppose they said there's nothing we can do for you, because one day Ron told me I was going back to Port Augusta. That was good. That wasn't the last I seen of my helper, Ron Kernick. Next time was at the Institute for the Blind in Adelaide.

So the same old lady came back and picked me up and took me to the train. She left me alone on a seat in a little room, a compartment I think they call it. At some railway station we stopped. I was just looking out the window, and right there, on another train, was a mob of horses. "Yahooo!" I said, "Fuck-inell!" I just looked and looked and I was feeling really good. When we got back to Port Augusta, she got me a taxi and gave the driver a piece of paper. He took me to a missionary at Umewarra Mission. The missionary took me to this fella by the name of Ray Boland and told him to look after me.

There were a lot of Aboriginal people speaking different languages at Umewarra: Arrernte from Alice Springs way; Arapanna from around Marree in South Australia; Yankunytjatjara and Pitjantjatjara; and I suppose Andnamathana too, from the Flinders Ranges. I could see some little houses and a church: a stone church. There was another building over a small sandhill I found out was the dormitory, where the kids went to school. The store and the missionaries' houses were there too. So I started living at Umewarra. I was a mission boy then.

Leslie Lester was still around, and one day he said to me: "Hey, *tjitji awai*. It's Sunday. We gotta go to church." That really frightened me. I didn't want to go to church. I didn't know anything about what went on there. I saw Ray Boland. He was all dressed up – suit and tie, white shirt. And I was just hiding out. They all went into this stone building, and I can hear the organ playing. Of course, I didn't know what it was.

Every day we'd go to the mission store and they give us a packet of Weetbix, a packet of sausages, tea and sugar, jam and butter. Once a week, a little blue bus would come from the mission and pick me up at Ray Boland's place to go for a check-up at the eye clinic. There were all these nice-looking Aboriginal girls on the bus, but I'd just keep my head down. I was too shy to talk to them – just a shy and skinny kid, one of those girls told me years later. Most days, I'd just walk around. I used to go the mission houses and I'd see the dormitories where the boys and girls lived – all nice and dressed up with coloured clothes. I still had my gaberdines, western shirt, high-heeled boots. And I'd see Leslie, and he'd keep telling me that what a good place the mission was.

Ray Boland was good to me and we'd go to the pictures in

town sometimes. But I didn't want to stay there. I didn't like the mission. Then, one day walking around the sandhills I saw him – my *tjamu*, one of my grandfathers, Kupinanya. He was a proper old man and I remembered him from travelling around Wallatina and Iwantja. He had a little camp with his daughter, Eileen, under a big umbrella bush. So I went back to Ray Boland's place, rolled up my swag, and went to the sandhills. Never told him where I was going.

He was a bit funny, my *tjamu*. Just a short fella, one old Yankunytjatjara fella with white whiskers. I never knew what he was doing in Port Augusta. That night, when I was lying in my swag, he gets up, takes all his clothes off, and then puts his pyjamas on. In the sandhills, the old bastard! He'd do that all the time, wherever we were camping. But it was good with him, and I was glad to be away from the mission. "You all right, *tjamu*. *Palya*?" And he'd say, "Yes, grandson, I'm all right."

Ray Boland dobbed on me, he went and told the missionaries I had pissed off. So when I turned up next day for my Weetbix and sausages and the rest of it, this missionary really dressed me down. I didn't know what he was on about. He had his hands on his hips, talking proper English, and I thought, "Oh, he's wild, this one." I just stood there with my head down, shuffling my feet, and all I wanted was the sausages and to get out of there. He finally gave them to me, but I didn't change. I went right back to my *tjamu*.

Our camp started getting big then. Two other people and their kids arrived from Andamooka. They knew Pingkai, my mother, so my *tjamu* told me they were another uncle and mother of mine. And then a young couple came in. I think she was a part-Aboriginal woman, married to this Aboriginal fella from Marree or Finnis Springs somewhere.

I was still going to the clinic every week to see Dr Thompson. I'd come out from the sandhills in the morning, wash my face, and stand by the road for the blue bus. But I still didn't know what was wrong with me. Dr Thompson never said, so I used to worry Leslie all the time: "Hey, brother. When am I going back to Oodnadatta?" And he'd say: "Oh, they say to wait a while longer. They want to keep an eye on you. Just hang on." But they never did anything. Anyway, one day Leslie comes up to me and says: "Yeah, all right. They say you can go back now."

Leslie wanted to stay behind, but my *tjamu* and his daughter were going with me. At the mission, they gave me a little blue ticket, and when we got to the train, this fella punched a hole in it and gave it back to me. They put us in this old rubbish carriage with a waterbag hanging outside. I think old Kupinanya was lost, sort of, like me. He just sat on the floor, train going along, just myall way. Me and my *tjamu*, on the train to Oodnadatta.

When we got back, I was still camping with my *tjamu* and his daughter. In the daytime, I'd just walk around the town. The kids would follow me and sing out: "Hey, whaddya you camp with that old man for? He'll give you grey hair, you know. You gotta keep away from old men." I'd just tell them: "Hey, get lost. He's my *tjamu*, poor thing. I'm sticking with him." Then this Aboriginal woman noticed me and I got an idea she was sort of looking after me. She would feed me, and one day she gave me threepence so I could get ice-cream. They called her Sheila and I think she was my relative somehow.

I was getting to know more Anangu in the town. Me and my *tjamu* would go and sit and have a yarn with all the old Southern Arrernte and Arapanna men, people like Jack Yampi and Dick Carrol. There was quite a few of them, but they're all finished now. That old Arrernte fella was there too, the one that helped me in the stock camp when I went blind. He was working for the National Railway then. And sometimes I used to see this one part-Aboriginal fella dressed up really smart, and I'd go to the camp behind the hospital and listen to him playing guitar. He used to sing old Hank Williams songs, ones like "I got lovesick blues" and all that.

One day all the men were behind this shed, so I went over to have a look at what was going on. That part-Aboriginal fella was there, singing with his guitar, and the others were playing two-up. I could see they were gambling for a lot of money:

Left:
Kanytji and
Pingkai
*(Photo:
Lester family)*

Bottom:
Dick Lander
*(Photo:
Mertie Lander)*

Top: The mail truck from Oodnadatta loading wool at
Ernabella c. 1945–46.
(Photo: Bill Lennon)

Bottom: The house at Sailors Well, Wallatina.
(Photo: Mertie Lander)

Top: Everard Park (Mimili) in 1948.
(Photo: Frank Halls)

Bottom: Camel wagon at Granite Downs.
(Photo: Bruce Evans)

Top:
Cattle branding at Granite
Downs Station.
(Photo: Bruce Evans)

Left:
Jim Davey,
"Old Ironbark".
(Photo Bruce Evans)

Top: Cattle work. Brian Norris drafting cattle on Granite Downs Station.

Bottom: Branding cattle on Granite Downs Station.
(Photos taken from the film "Cattleman's Day" 1961, reproduced courtesy of Ray Beale)

Top: "All day it rained." Flooded creek at Wallatina
in the 1940s.
(Photo: Mertie Lander)

Bottom: Colebrook Home.
(Photo: Eric Finck)

Top: Yami with Brother
McGowan, 12 March
1957: the first day at
Colebrook Home.
(Photo: Eric Finck)

Left: First day at the
Blind Institute.
(Photo: Eric Finck)

Top: Robin Percy selling stores at Granite Downs
in 1965.
(Photo: Robin Percy)

Bottom: Kanytji and Pingkai, and Shannon and
his wife Puna c. 1965.
(Photo: Robin Percy)

Aborigines In P.S.A. Service

Above: Outside Colebrook Home, 25 November 1961.
(Photo: Eric Finck)

Left: *The Advertiser*, 15 July 1963.

Bottom: Yami and Lucy married at Grote Street, 11 June 1966.
(Photo: Eric Finck)

Aboriginal soloists and a mission choir provided the music at the Maughan Church PSA yesterday.

Among the soloists was singer and guitarist Jimmy Lester, 22, of Oodnadatta, who is blind.

National Aborigines Day observance was mentioned in churches of nearly every denomination yesterday.

ABOVE—Jimmy Lester playing at Maughan Church yesterday afternoon.

Top: Lucy, Leroy and Yami in Adelaide.
(Photo: Lester family)

Left: Pastor Douglas Nicholls, later Sir Douglas Nicholls.
(Photo: SA Museum, photographer unknown)

Top: Charles Perkins being removed from Moree swimming pool during the Freedom Bus Rides. *(Photo: News Limited)*

Left to Right: Ringo Tjapilya, Yami with Rosemary and Shannon at Achilpa Street, Alice Springs, c. 1973. *(Photo: Lester family)*

Top: Yami with Jim Downing at the IAD buildings on South Terrace. *(Photo: IAD files)*

Bottom: At Mimili, June 1978. Left to right: Leroy, Rosemary, Yami (nursing Karina) and Lucy.
(Photo: Lester family)

Top: An artificial insemination workshop, part of IAD's Rural Extension Program; Yami is third from left.
(Photo: IAD files)

Bottom: Students from Lewis and Clarke College, Portland, Oregon, USA, attending a cross-culture course in September 1981. Yami is kneeling at front right, next to Pat Dodson. Peter Willis is first on the right in the back row.
(Photo: IAD files)

Top: On the bus going to Adelaide. First two rows left to right:
Tiger, Mr Mick, Dickie Minyintiri, Larry, Sandy Mutjun, Tony
Tjamiwa, unidentified and Hadleyka tjamu.
(Photo: the Advertiser*)*

Bottom: Then Premier of South Australia, David Tonkin,
hands over freehold title to Anangu on 4 November 1981 near
Ernabella.
(Photo: IAD files)

Top: Yami and Reggie Uluṟu on Handback Day

Bottom: Handback Day – Yami on stage with, from left to right, Professor Ovington, Clyde Holding and Sir Ninian Stephen.

(Photos: Australian Institute of Aboriginal and Torres Strait Islander Studies)

Top: Yami, Lucy and Richard Bradshaw, right, departing for
London from Alice Springs airport, June 1984.
(Photo: IAD files)

Bottom: Pingkai and Kanytji, Yami's parents, view the Totem
One test site at Emu Field, with Jim McClelland.
(Photo: Bryan Charlton)

they'd drawn a ring on the ground and it had a lot of green notes inside, pound notes. One of them would throw two coins in the air, and somebody'd sing out, "Heads!" or maybe "Tails!" I was standing there watching them when this policeman came around the corner: "Righto, you fellas! Break it up!" They all stopped playing then, and he said, "Pick up the money, too, or I'll take the lot." Or something like that. Before he left, he was talking to Dick Carrol, and he told me that there was a job for me starting tomorrow.

I was going out with these two contractors, two brothers. I think their name was James or Jones and they used to put up windmills and tanks on the stations around there. Next morning I got my little swag. I still had all my gear inside – leggings, stockwhip, spurs, and all that – and went with them, west. They were going to Utunungatjara, the place Jim Davey called Alice Bore. And all the way there I kept thinking: "Oh, this is all right. I'm getting close to Granite Downs. No worries, Wallatina Kid."

Straight north and over the sandhills from Utunungatjara, Jim Davey had put in a new bore while I was away. When we got there, I could see cattle, and there were some short horses grazing near the diesel pump and water trough. They didn't have the Granite Downs brand on them – that little revolver on the right shoulder – and I reckon they must've come from Jim Davey's other station. There were four Anangu there, but I can't remember their names. One fella was camping with his wife and her friend, and the other bloke was single. The two men were there to help us put up the new windmill and tank.

There was another whitefella with us, and me and him would go to Alice Bore in a big army truck to get gravel for the cement. We would take it back to that new Nicka Bore, start up the cement-mixer, mix it up with sand and water, pour it into the holes for the four legs of the windmill and make a base for the new tank.

One day, on the way to Alice Bore, we saw this Land Rover coming down the track. There was a whitefella driving it and a part-Aboriginal fella sitting in the passenger side. We stopped, and they came alongside. The part-Aboriginal fella got out and it was my brother, Hughie Cullinan. And he was really good to me. "Hey, *wai?* What's happening? Where you been?" He was taking the mob of horses from Nicka Bore back to Granite Downs. He said, "Hey, forget this contract work. It's rubbish. Come with me back to Granite Downs, back to the station." But I wanted to finish. "Yeah. OK, brother. I'll go back. But I'll finish this job first. When they pay me, that's it, I'll go. I'll go when I get my pay." But I never made it, and I never got paid either. And since then I've always had it in my mind that if I'd gone with him things would have been different. I don't know, maybe I've got no good reason to think that, but it's how I feel.

After Hughie took the horses back, we kept working, until one day that north wind started to blow. It's always been an evil wind for me. And it was really hot. Those whitefellas said it was too hot to work, so they just rested under a bough shed. I was camping a little bit away from the others with that single bloke. All day that evil north wind kept blowing, same north wind, and that night I didn't feel the best. When I woke up in the morning, I couldn't see. I opened my eyes, and I couldn't see the bastard.

So they didn't work. That day it was hot again, and around dinner time that single fella I was with went to talk to the whitefellas. They decided to take me into Oodnadatta that afternoon in the little ute they had. They put me in the back. I was in pain and I was crying.

When we got to Oodnadatta, that same sister came over to the truck and seen me lying there. She put some drops in my eyes. When I opened them, I could just see the moon, a big moon going down in the west. It was just about the last thing I ever saw. They helped me out and put me in that same little hospital, in a bed away from everybody else. A special place for me, where they put the blackfellas.

And I stayed there and waited for the Ghan to take me to Port Augusta again. While I'd been out working, Dick Carrol and some of the other men got into trouble with the police. They were going to Port Augusta too. The police were going to look after them on the train and the prisoners were going to look after me.

They did the same thing when we got there: took me from the station to the hospital. All my mates on the train left me and went to Greenbush lockup. Dr Thompson had a look at my eye, and the same day they put me in an ambulance with a white girl – she was pretty sick too. We were going all the way to Adelaide.

From the ambulance, they took me to some sort of room where this doctor opened my eyes and looked at them with a torch. And I saw one red light. I'll never forget that red light – I couldn't see their faces or anything. Just this one red light and it was the last thing I ever saw. I don't know who signed for the operation, but they removed my eye soon after – the one I was using to get around. It was sore and, I don't know, there might've been a good reason for it. Maybe it was going to burst – might be no good for my brains. They never told me. All I know is that they removed my eye.

That's the end of the story. The first part anyway.

ngampu – balls, testicles
muntawa – oh really, oh yes

Another education

I was still in the hospital when I found out I might not be going back. A man came to see me there. His name was Mr Samuels, Pastor L. J. Samuels. I'll never forget that man. He had found himself in almost the same circumstances as me. He became blind when he was twelve years old. When I knew him he was secretary of the United Aboriginal Mission.

Pastor Samuels talked to me, but I couldn't understand what he was saying most of the time. He'd ask me a question, and I might say "Yes", then he'd ask again and wait for me. And I would think: "Hmn. Last time I said yes, I think this time I'll say no." It was up and down like that: yes and no. He'd put it down on the paper what I said. I thought this was dangerous for me, this writing down. But Pastor Samuels was helping me, arranging for me to learn new things. Of course, I didn't understand that then. I thought my life was finished. All I wanted was to be a stockman. But although I hated it at the time, I am glad now that he arranged for me to go to the Colebrook Home and to learn things that I needed later on. So I have had two lots of education in my life.

Looking back now, I realise that he organised for this fella, Mr Finck, to come and get me. The day Mr Finck came, they got clothes for me and dressed me up. Never wore socks before, and it was the first time I had underpants on, and I felt strange. They put me in a car, and he drove me to a place called Colebrook Home. The road went winding up through the Adelaide Hills, and I got to feeling carsick. I didn't know where I was. All I kept thinking about was going back to Mimili, where my family were. I just wanted to go back.

When Mr Finck stopped the car, I could hear a lot of kids, a lot of younger boys and girls, and they were all just talking

English. Mr Finck – I found out later he was the superintendent – arranged a room for me with two boys about my age. One lad was Graham McKenzie – he still gives me a ring now and then. And the other was Georgie Turner, a lad from Andamooka. Poor thing, he's finished now. Like Pastor Samuels, he helped me to get used to being blind. Georgie became my friend and my interpreter. When Georgie saw me, he said, "Hey, *tjuu*." He spoke to me in Yankunytjatjara! And it just made my day. Georgie was my interpreter. "Sorry, *tjuu*. You won't be able to go back. You won't be able to go back to Mimili. Ever. They're going to keep you here and teach you new things. You'll go to the Blind Institute in North Adelaide. Learn to make things, you know, what blind people do." I cried. I wanted to go back to Mimili. And Georgie said again: "Sorry. That's what's going to happen."

I asked Georgie in Yankunytjatjara: "I had an eye to see with, and they took it out. *Nyaaku*? Why?" Georgie couldn't tell me, of course, and Mr Finck didn't say anything. So my interpreter said, "Oh, maybe your eye was really bad or… " You know, like that.

"But what about… Will I be able to see again?"

"*Wiya*. You're blind. That's it. No eyes. Finished."

So I started crying again. So that was it? Georgie said: "Oh, we gonna – you know – teach you how to, how to walk around with somebody. Get strong. Don't worry, I'll take you around."

Georgie did that. And when he was away at high school during the day, I used to go for walks down the road with this Englishman. He was a handyman around the place and all the boys and girls called him Brother McGowan. But it was just no good for a while. I'd lie in bed and think about horse riding. I'd think about Mimili; I'd think about Wallatina; I'd think about Granite Downs. And about Hughie Cullinan, Ginger, and Wallace. I used to cry, just thinking about it.

I found out that Colebrook Home was for younger part-Aboriginal kids. I was too old to be there, but they didn't have any other place for a person like me. So they were going to let me stay – for a little while. But there wasn't much to do. One day Mr Finck came around and it looked like he had a job for me. He had a bag of potatoes and I had to pick them out – put them in a box. Out of the bag and into the box. So I'd be doing that, just working with my hands. And waiting for Georgie to come home from school so I could sit down and talk. When he got back and changed from his school clothes, we'd walk around inside the fence of Colebrook Home. Other kids would be playing cricket or kicking the footie. And he'd sit down and talk to me. We'd have a big talk, then he'd get up and have a kick. He was a really good mate to me.

Sometimes I'd talk to the other kids, but most of them didn't have the language. I remember this one little kid from Yalata and his name was Dennis Matthews. He spoke only English then. They used to call him *maṟu* – I suppose it means something like "blackfella". And he'd always come up to me and ask, "You know why?" And I'd say, "Yeah." And he'd say, "Why?" Nothing else. I used to think: "Now what am I going to say now? What's he saying 'You know why' all the time for, the bastard?"

I think Colebrook was all right for young people from a long way out to get an education. They came from the River Country and from places up north too – Marree and Oodnadatta. It was a good home, I suppose: good bed to sleep, and the others had school to go to. But they had pretty strict rules and I didn't like that part; I didn't think it was fair on the kids.

Sundays were the worst. The Lord's Day, they'd call it. We had Sunday school in the morning, and in the afternoon we had to stay in our rooms and read the Bible. Not even play with a ball. We had to be quiet and, of course, I couldn't read, so I'd just lie in bed. It was really, really boring. One time, one of the older boys came back to Colebrook to stay a while. He'd been a ringer Marree way and was having a holiday in Adelaide. It was Sunday, and we're all there, supposed to be reading the Bible, and that fella came in and starts talking to me. He had this balloon in his hand, tossing it up and down. Then the superintendent passed by and saw us. He just told us off: said it was the Lord's Day and we can't be playing on the Lord's Day. I thought he was off his head.

It was like that. And if the Home helped some people get an education I also remember them saying: "When I turn sixteen, I'm goin' to leave this place and I'm finished with church. I've had enough." So instead of wanting to go to church, they were set against the church. They had a gutful of it. Same with the girls. I think that's what happened to most of them. They left thinking like that.

I was getting stronger. Georgie and Graham were telling me I should learn Braille, reading by feeling dots. They'd say: "Ah, later on Mr Samuels is gonna send you to that place where other blind people are. They're clever and they make things. You're gonna go there and learn the same things." When the time came, Mr Samuels arranged for me to be picked up by this fella whose name was Mr Radcliffe and taken to the Institute for the Blind. He went to the same church as we went to for Sunday school, and he lived in Blackwood, next door to Eden Hills where Cole-brook Home was.

I remember the first day I turned up for work. They gave me lunch to take and a bag with overalls that Mr Samuels had got for me. After Mr Radcliffe dropped me off at the Institute, the caretaker showed me a locker, and I got the overalls out and put them on. Then he took me downstairs where I met other blind people working in the different factories.

For me the start was brush-making. I didn't know it then, but they put me there for three months' trial. If that didn't work out, they were going to try me out on the baskets or mats or feather dusters or maybe mops. They had all these different materials, some from horsehair and other things, to make the brushes and brooms. My first job was to get to know them. So they sat me down across from this other fella and between us was a long bench. I had to pick up a bundle of the material from its drawer, pick out the right amount to fit into one of the holes in what they called the stock – that's the base of the broom or brush – then knock the material I had on a glass so it's even, and fit it into the stock so it's a tight fit. You'd have to pick the right size: too small and it would come out; too big and it wouldn't fit the hole. So, maybe for a week or more, I worked like that. Not making the brooms, but learning. They talked about working with the hot pitch later.

Then they'd teach me to dip that bundle of material I'd put in the holes in the stock into this cold tray. There were two strikers attached to the tray: one facing me, and one on the other side for the person across from me. When I got used to that, they started me on the hot pitch. We'd dip the material in that, wipe off some if you got too much, then tie a knot, dip it again, and put it into the stock. We'd have to be careful or we'd burn our fingers dipping too far, and I did that lots of times. When we put it in the stock, we'd spread it out, so it wasn't standing straight up like soldiers. We'd cover the wood so you couldn't see it. There was a rack behind us, where we could put maybe a dozen finished ones. Then a bloke came along and took them to a machine to trim up the top. Then it's finished. Broom or brush is ready to go. All the handles would be in the next room. When people buy the broom in the showroom at the Institute, they buy the handles, and stick them together themselves.

I did that for thirteen years and ten months.

There were one hundred and fifteen blind people at the Institute: young and old, German, Italian, French, Scotsman, Welshmen, Australians. All different languages. There were a lot of Australians, but I was the only Australian Anangu. And we were all working there. The women would make brushes too, not with the hot pitch, but with fine copper wire. And they'd make shoe brushes, brushes for polishing floors, and special ones too, like brushes for sweeping out the inside of train carriages. They'd all be together doing that in a special room. Some people would start on the brooms, but they didn't like the hot pitch, so they'd be put on making different baskets, or making mats. Next door to us they were making feather dusters, mops, and glass washboards. I remember old Mrs Cullinan had one of those washboards. And later on I was making this special broom to clean out cattle troughs, and I thought: "Oh, shit! I used one like this at Granite Downs!" And they were terrible things to make. Sixty-four holes in the stock and the material for the brush was six inches long. I think they get it from South America. I don't know what it is, but it's hard, and we got sore knuckles making those trough brooms. We didn't like making them at all.

For the first four and a half years, from 1957 to 1961, I was living at Colebrook. Weekdays, I'd get up early, maybe seven o'clock, and Mr Radcliffe would come and pick me up. He'd get me to the Institute to start work at eight. Sometimes I'd be late: ten past or quarter past maybe. Knock off at quarter past four, then get cleaned up, go down to the back and clean up with special industrial soap. That black pitch had a very strong smell, and it'd get on your hands and in your hair and it'd stick on your clothes. Then I'd change out of my overalls, get my white stick, walk down with somebody to the corner across from the Children's Hospital, and he'd put me on the bus. I'd go down South Terrace and meet one of Mr Radcliffe's working boys, and he'd take me around to Mr Radcliffe's panel-beating shop. And I'd sit there waiting for him to finish. By the time I got home, it would be half-past seven, or sometimes eight o'clock. Then I'd have dinner that they'd saved for me. When I finished, I'd go to my room and all my mates would sing out: "Hey, Lester!" They'd be still playing or doing their homework. And we'd have a yarn. Then I'd have a shower, go to bed, and start again the next day.

When I started working at the Institute, I didn't like it. And the more I worked there, the more I hated it. But there was nothing else for me to do. In the 1960s I was getting really sick of it and looking for something else. I knew of other blind people who left and worked at the Holden factory, or Chrysler's, or making aeroplane wings. They worked at Kodak, too, developing films. One blind fella was making baskets at home. He liked to do gardening, so he could do that and make baskets too.

It wasn't always bad working there. Oh, we'd have a few laughs sometimes. I remember some of us used to knock off before the bell, we were doing the wrong thing, you know, sneaking out early. One day the manager sent a letter around, read us the riot act. Told us knock-off time was quarter past four; it wasn't fair to the others for some of us to leave early, and, besides, there was plenty of time to catch the bus. We'd blame each other: "Now, you started that, and you're making it hard for everybody else." Anyway, we'd say, "That's tomorrow, today is today!" And we'd all race off before the bell. There was one blind fella called Rocky who could play anything – piano, guitar, piano accordion – and he was really quick. Just as we were going upstairs to get cleaned up, he'd be coming down. When he got to the bottom of the stairs he ran into this bloke coming the other way and said to him, "Get out of my bloody way." The fella stepped aside, and Rocky took off down the laneway with his white cane tapping. Turned out that fella was the manager!

And we used to play tricks on each other all the time. There were two totally blind fellas working there, and they used to go to the Cathedral pub around the corner at lunch. One time they got a couple of bottles of beer each, brought them back and hid them in one of those troughs of water where the cane was soaked for baskets. They didn't know it, but this part-sighted fella was watching them all the time. At three o'clock smoko, they went down to the wash-house to have a beer. Popped them open and went to have a drink, but there was nothing but water. That's the kind of thing that used to happen. But mostly it was pretty boring for us at the Blind Institute.

And on weekends, there wasn't much to do at Colebrook Home either. Once a month we had to take everything out from the room, take a brush and a bucket of water, and scrub the floor on our hands and knees. Other Saturdays we'd sweep up and tidy our rooms, sit down and listen to the radio. I had a record-player too. I wanted to get rock and roll, things like that, but all they had was hymns. So boring! I used to listen to this big baritone fella, George Beverley Shay, singing "Marching Forward", or something like that. And I'd be saying "hear, hear" on my hands and knees and go on scrubbing the floor.

Sometimes we'd listen to the football: Aussie Rules. But Mr Finck, the superintendent, never let us put on the races broadcast. "Put on this station," he'd say. He was very worried about us listening to a station with ads coming on. Only me, Graham, and Georgie had the radio anyway. Mr Finck wouldn't let the other kids sit down with us.

When the football came on, I wouldn't know any of the teams, so Georgie and Graham were teaching me: "You gotta barrack for the Redlegs." They told me their colours were red and blue. "That's the team you gotta barrack for, all right? You know: Up the Redlegs! Come on, put your hands up. *Minakatingu.*" So I did and that was it. I was stuck with it. So I barracked for Redlegs. And they'd say, "Oh, you'll meet all the players and all that. They're good players, you know." It was the 1958 or 1959 season, and there was this one Norwood Rover, Peter Vivian. Georgie'd say: "Now, he's a good footballer. Now you say it: Peter Vivian." And I'd say his name after him. He'd teach me all the players' names like that. And he said: "If anyone asks you who you barrack for, say 'Redlegs'! When I'm not around that's what you say. Can you say Redlegs?" Georgie Turner, my interpreter.

I'd been at the Institute for a while when I decided I wanted to learn English. So I went to see Pat McCulloch, the Public Relations Officer. He's passed away now, but he became a very good friend of mine. He asked me, "Can you speak any English?" I told him I couldn't, not properly. "Well, to teach you English, first I gotta teach you Braille." We did that for four years: half an hour each day, Monday to Friday. Sometimes we'd miss out – he'd get sick or he might be away or I might get sick – but that's what we did and we had a lot of fun together. He'd start me on "a" for apple, "b" for bat, "c" for cat and so on. And he'll ask me what an apple is, and what's a bat. It's a cricket bat, I'd say. I learnt about numbers too. How to count – one, two, three and all that. And he'd teach me how to read and write, all in Braille. Later on, he'd give me new words. He wasn't a schoolteacher, he was just helping me. One day he was teaching me "oa" words, ones that sound like "boat", "coat", "coax". He'd say it and I'll say it, then he'll ask me do I know what it means. "Boat? Oh, yeah, that's that big thing that floats on the water. And coat? It's what a man or woman wears." Then he'd say, "Maybe you don't know this one, but do you know

99

what 'coax' is?" No worries: "Oh, yeah, yeah. I know that. You get them in the bottles!" And he'd laugh, and tell me the meaning. But I still can't remember what "coax" means.

One day he said: "Look, this is as far as I know. This is as far as I can take you." So he rang around adult education centres to try and see if they could do more for me. But they didn't have a special course for a person like me. "Sorry, friend," he said. "I'm not a teacher, but it's been really good." And I said, "Thanks mate, I've learned a lot. I'll use what I learned from you." And that's what I've been doing. I picked up a lot from other people since then, but he started me off.

When he was teaching me about English, he used to talk about a blind orchestra and about blind cricket. He said that during the war, the Institute had had a blind cricket team. I was interested, so he told me about his other mate called Allan Wood: "Well, look. I'll get Woodsie to see if he can find the stumps and the old bat in the shed. Might still be some there." When Woodsie got them out, he said that he could make me a cricket ball. They use a cane ball with a bell inside for blind cricket. Woodsie was the foreman in the cane shop, so he made me two of them. And he got the wood-turning bloke to make three new stumps and sit them on a block of wood with a little bell hanging behind the middle stump.

Then they showed me how they used to play. Allan Wood was bowling and Pat was wicket-keeper. Woodsie said to me: "We'll let you bat. You stand there. Listen to the ball and try to hit it." He'd bowl to me and I'd miss it. It wasn't easy. And Pat, with his big belly, would try to catch it, but the ball was passing him all the time. But I got the idea, and I liked it.

So I'd start asking other blind fellas if they were interested. At first, they'd just make excuses: "Ah, no. It's too hot!" Like that. But I kept on talking to them. I could write Braille by then, and I was getting some names. I went around the workshop, starting with the Brush Shop, Mop Shop, Mat Shop, then go to the Coconut Matting Shop and the Basket Shop. In the end I got ten names, enough to play. I told them they had to pick a captain, and they did that. Then I told them what Pat McCulloch and

Woodsie showed me. I got Woodsie to come down and teach us all how to play. So that's how the Blind Cricket Team at the Blind Institute got going again.

We'd have a lot of good times. I remember one day we were practising at LeFevre Terrace in North Adelaide, not far from some horse stables and a riding school. There was five of us blind fellas there, and I was batsman. I'd hit the ball, and they'd have to get to it before it stopped rolling and making that rattling noise. But they must've been slow that day, because they kept losing it. So we had to wait while they were out there feeling around for the ball. Sometimes you'd find horse droppings and you'd throw that instead. Anyway, we didn't know it, but when they're trying to find the ball, this horse walked up and got somewhere between me and the bowler. When they finally found it, the bowler says to me, "Right. Ready?" He takes a bit of a run, throws the ball, and hit that horse right in the guts. All we heard was this big fart, then he bolted. "Ah, shit! Look out!"

We had to find a team to play against us. I went to Pat McCulloch to ask him what teams they used to play against, and he said: "Oh, we used to play against church groups, Adelaide Fire Brigade, and Lions Club or Rotary Club." And I said, "But what do they do? How do they play?" "Well, they're fully-sighted, so they play our rules: if they're a proper right-hander, we make them bat left-handed. And if they're proper left-handers, they play right-handed."

I started with the Brighton Garden Church. After our first game they used to look forward to playing us every summer. They'd bowl underarm to us, and they'd bat with the wrong hand. We started playing Saturday afternoons, and then we'd play Sunday too, but the church people wouldn't come on Sunday. It was good fun, and I'd look forward to it. We never won, but we just got stronger and stronger. One day I said to the others: "Hey, Pat was telling me that when they had a team before, they used to play Victoria, New South Wales and Queensland." So we wrote a Braille letter to the Melbourne Blind Institute and told them we wanted a match. They had four teams in Melbourne. They wrote back and said that because we were just starting up, they'd send their second-best team. And they thrashed us. One of the pubs in Adelaide gave a lot of money for a trophy. The manager's name was Arthur Stone, so they called it the Arthur Stone Trophy. And it was beautiful: three cricket stumps and a bloke on the top standing with a bat. They took it to Victoria and we never won it back! Just like the America's Cup. Gone!

We went to Sydney and I think we finished fourth on the table, but I got a little cup for best bowler from South Australia. Later on, after I left the Institute, they'd go interstate and play in the cricket carnivals every two years. And they would still give me a game while I was in Alice Springs. I think it was out of kindness, because they said it was my idea to get it going again. I was happy to play thirteenth man – I didn't want to push somebody out that'd been training all the time. But they said, "No, no. You got the game."

I was still at the Colebrook Home when we started the cricket. Then Georgie and Graham left as soon as they turned sixteen, and I wanted to leave too. Before I went to Colebrook a couple worked there called Mr and Mrs Hill. They were now living at Nova Gardens, not far from Brighton, and they had three or four adopted sons. Howard Hill worked for the Education Department. One day when he was at Colebrook he asked me if I would like to go to their place for a weekend. I did, and I had a good time. It was different from Colebrook. On the way back to the Home he said: "Look, Jim. If you're interested, we'd very much like to have you as a boarder. If you think you're too old to live at Colebrook and you want to get away, you can live with us and have a different lifestyle." And I said, "Are you offering me?" By this time I can talk that second language. "Yeah, the offer is there." So I told Mr Samuels I was going to board with Mr and Mrs Hill. The Colebrook people weren't very happy about it, but I told them: "Look, I want it. I want to go." I wasn't much more than a big kid, maybe nineteen or twenty, and I left.

I packed up all my gear and went to live with the Hills. I paid my board from my Institute wages. I'd catch the train from Brighton to Adelaide and then catch a bus to work. Leaving

Colebrook and living with the Hills was the best thing that happened to me.

I was going to the Brighton Church of Christ then, and Mr and Mrs Hill went to the Church of England. They didn't mind which church I went to as long as I went to church. Mr Hill was good on the piano and organ and he conducted the boys' choir at his church.

Not long after I went to live in Brighton, in about 1961 or 1962, Mr and Mrs Finck left Colebrook, and they were looking for another missionary couple to take over. They found someone, but that didn't last long, so Mr and Mrs Hill decided to go back for twelve months. I said to them: "All right, do that. I'll look after your house. You can rent it to me." They said, "Well, it's only for twelve months." So Tjilpi Hill left the Education Department and the Hills went back to being missionaries again.

The Hills had a good friend who, in the early days, used to cook for the boys and girls at Colebrook Home. Her name was Sophie Bishop, but everybody at the church just used to call her Auntie Soph. She was seventy-six years old. Mr Hill told me: "Maybe I can get Sophie Bishop to come and give you a hand, Jim. She can do the cooking and a bit of laundry for you." She was an old woman, but she was still active, still driving a car. He talked to her and she came. She stayed in one of the rooms in the house and would drive me to the train in the mornings. And it worked well.

Around the time when Mr and Mrs Hill were coming back, I said to them, "You know, I like the idea of having a house to myself. I'm going to go look for a place." I'd saved up a little bit. A good mate of mine, Graham Thomas, and his parents helped me to look around. We found a house in North Brighton — 4 Cecilia Street. It was small: two bedrooms, kitchen area, sitting room, and a dining room you could turn into another bedroom. So I went to the bank for a loan and I got it. And Auntie Soph said to me: "Oh, I guess I'll come and help you for a little while, but you'll have to find a nice wife soon. I'm getting old." When Mr and Mrs Hill left Colebrook, I was already living at Cecilia Street.

So I had a new house, a job, and a new life I suppose, in Adelaide. But I was still thinking of my family; I still wanted to go up north to see my parents. I often asked the Welfare bloke for the far north, Don Busbridge, but every time he'd say, "Sorry, I can't take you. There's no room, full." Then one day in 1965 a lovely woman by the name of Sister Dot Forbes (she's passed away now) rang Auntie Soph and said she had room to take me back. I later found out that she also knew that I'd lost my brother, and the only one I had left now was Shannon. Sister Forbes was worried that I'd get a shock, and she wanted my family to tell me. Auntie Soph nearly told me, but she'd promised not to say anything.

Sister Forbes picked me up and drove me to Port Augusta, stayed overnight, then next day we went all the way to Coober Pedy. She was the nurse and Welfare worker for Aboriginal people – you know, all my relatives – living at Granite Downs and Mimili. I think she went to Amata too. A young fella by the name of Robin Percy was a Patrol Officer for Welfare then, and he worked with her. Robin met us at the Welfare Office in Coober Pedy, and he drove me out to look for Kanytji's camp. We saw one young fella standing there, so Robin pulled up and said: "G'day. Where's Kanytji and Pingkai?"

"Ah, they're gone that way."

Robin pointed to me and said, "You know this bloke?"

"Yeah. He's my brother."

It was Shannon! And we just hugged each other, you know. So we all got into Robin's car and went to look for them. Their camp was just an old motor car with canvas over it, sitting in an open flat. Not many trees in Coober Pedy. My parents weren't there, so Robin left my string bag with food in it and went back to his office, and Shannon and me waited for them.

When my parents came back, they could see under the car – one, two, three, four legs. Two people sitting on the tailgate. So they hurried around and as soon as they saw me they just cried. And I cried. Then they started talking, and I just couldn't understand what they were saying! I'd lost my language. Auntie

Eileen Brown, my mother's younger sister, heard us and she came over from her camp, then they were all crying and happy. It took me four days to pick up my Yankunytjatjara again. And I promised myself then: "I'm never gonna let the language go away. I'm gonna hang onto it."

I spent sixteen days in Coober Pedy with my mother and father and my bros, Shannon. I found out that they'd been looking for me, asking Welfare people where I was. It was Dot Forbes and Robin Percy that worked it out for us. Robin had picked up my family at Iwantja and taken them to Coober Pedy to wait for me. So I'd go to their camp every day – they'd moved it closer to the reserve – and at night I'd sleep at Robin's house. When I got back to Adelaide, I bought a second-hand tape-recorder, and would send tapes up to my mother and father. We'd communicate like that.

Before I went up to Coober Pedy, I'd gone to an eye doctor, David Tonkin. I had a lot to do with him later, when he became Premier of South Australia. He wanted to perform a corneal graft on one of my eyes. I told him that I'd like to do it after I saw my family, and he said that was all right – it could wait. I went to the hospital for the operation in the middle of October. But it didn't work, I was still blind.

I was on my back for about eighteen days. And they were good to me. The nurses would take me around in a wheelchair, wheel me outside, or put me by a window and say, "Here you go, Jim, you can sit down here and look through the window." You know, having fun with me. "Ah, you girls are mad." We'd carry on like that.

First couple of days I was in the hospital, this part-Aboriginal girl came to see me. She was from a girl's home called Millswood or Wiltja Hostel. She worked as an assistant matron there. Her name was Lucy Turner. She told me that on her day off she always went to the hospital to visit Ernabella people, especially those whose language was Yankunytjatjara. So we talked about Ernabella, and I said: "Yeah, well, I don't know Ernabella. I was at Mimili and Kenmore. But I know the Musgrave Ranges. I've seen them."

I found out that her situation was a bit like mine. Her father was a whitefella, Frank Butler, and he used to work for Frank Smith, the owner of Tieyon Station. She went down to Adelaide because the Presbyterian Board of Missions didn't really want what they called half-caste kids living at Ernabella. I really don't know why. I think they were embarrassed or something. So Charles Duguid – he was the doctor who started Ernabella Mission in the 1930s – said he'd take her. And they did. Mrs Duguid taught English to Lucy, like Pat McCulloch was teaching me.

Now, I didn't really know Lucy before then, but I knew some of her friends. I'd learnt the guitar while working at the Institute, and I used to travel around Adelaide playing and trying to sing. There was another girls' home, Tandira, and I used to see the Tandira girls a fair bit. They had a nice singing group going, and sometimes we'd be on the same concert. One girl there was June McInerney, Hughie Cullinan's niece. Another one was Linda Bush, a friend of Lucy's. Linda told Lucy about me, and how I was in the hospital. And that was how Lucy came to visit me.

After a few more days Lucy came again. They let me out of the hospital that weekend, and Bill Docking took me home. Lucy rang up and Auntie Soph answered the phone while I was asleep. When I woke up, Aunt Soph said, "Oh, that nice girl Lucy rang and I invited her for dinner." When Lucy came over, Auntie Soph said to us, "I'm still cooking, so why don't you two sit outside for a while." She made us a nice cold drink – I wasn't a beer drinker then – and we sat outside together, playing dominoes. I think Auntie Soph was trying everything; she didn't want to work any more.

That's how me and Lucy got friendly then. We fell in love and Auntie Soph was real happy. We wanted a short engagement, but we couldn't get married when we wanted. Both of us needed a birth certificate. Pastor Samuels had to agree for me to get married. A missionary had to decide. So we had to wait for the papers. I finally got them, and Dr Duguid arranged for Lucy's. We were married in June 1966. Proper whitefella style.

Our first son, Leroy, was born in 1967. For the few days that Lucy was in hospital, Auntie Sophie came to give me a hand. Then she went back to her rest home. Later on, when I was in Alice Springs, I went back to see her. She was very old then, poor thing.

I was still at the Blind Institute, still working, still playing cricket. But I was really sick of making brooms and was looking for a way to get out. One thing I had going for me was knowing my first language again, and I wanted to use it. So I started doing a bit of part-time interpreting. My first chance was at the courthouse in Port Augusta. The police had picked up this old fella near the railway line at Tarcoola. They charged him with something unusual he was doing. Poor thing, he was just a sick old man, something wrong with his head.

It was my first time in court. When the magistrate came in, I realised that I knew him. Stewart Cameron. He knew me too. He used to come up to Colebrook Home and see us when he was a barrister. He would take us for a ride in his car, a Ford Customline, it was. And Georgie and Graham, they used to tell me, "Best car is Ford." They'd say: "That Stewart Cameron, he's got the best car. He'll come and take us for a ride." Sure enough, he'd turn up, and we'd all get into his Ford. Graham and Georgie would ask him if they could drive, but he'd say, "No, no. Wait until you get your licence, you fellas."

Anyway, back in the courtroom, the magistrate didn't get to that old fella before they adjourned for morning tea. So he sent his clerk out to get me. When I got into his room, Stewart Cameron said: "Jim Lester! What are you doing here? I got a bit of a shock seeing you. I haven't seen your name here, but since I know you I can't hear your case."

"*Wiya*. I'm interpreting for that *tjilpi*."

"Oh, thank Christ! You want a cup of tea?"

So he gave me a cup of tea, then the clerk took me back to the court and we started again. When he called that old fella up I interpreted for him. He didn't send him to gaol. He just said, "You're all right this time," and sent him back. And I was thinking to myself: "Gee, I want to do more of this. It's better than sweatin' over the hot pitch!"

I put my name down for interpreting at the state Office for Aboriginal Affairs. John Miller was the boss then. Not long after, I got a second job, interpreting for this old lady in the hospital. She got hit on the head with a boomerang at Yalata, and it was pretty bad. They rang me up and took me to the operating theatre. They dressed me up with this gown and all that, and I went in to talk to her. I told her to breathe normally, just relax, before they put her asleep. Later on they called me back to see how the operation went. They wanted to know if her brains were all right, but they couldn't understand her, of course. So I talked to her and she talked to me, and I told the brain surgeon, Dr Trevor Turner: no worries, her speech is all right. That's all I had to do. Just talk to her.

I kept on doing that kind of work here and there. Then one Christmas, Lucy got a letter from this fella, Reverend Jim Downing. He was in Alice Springs at the time. There was a lot of news in the letter I didn't know much about, but one part really interested me. He said that interpreting was taking up too much of his time. It was a full-time job, and he had other work to do. He could speak Pitjantjatjara, a language a little bit like Yankunytjatjara. Maybe there was a chance for me.

What was in my mind was helping people, like Georgie Turner had helped me at Colebrook Home. I wasn't thinking about going back to the bush. I just thought if people like me were coming into Alice Springs hospital and having difficulties, I could help them. I knew what it's like when you can't communicate. In those early days when I was in the hospital, I used to worry a lot about my interviews with doctors and people like Mr Samuels, wondering about what they were saying, and what they were writing down. That's the kind of work I wanted. And I wanted to get out of the Institute.

I wasn't much involved with Aboriginal politics then, but my thinking was changing. At first I wanted to be sort of a missionary. I was at the Church of Christ and one person I had a lot of time for was a minister of the same church, but in Melbourne. He was an Aboriginal man by the name of Pastor Doug

Nicholls. He used to speak at the National Aborigines Day cele-brations. He would tell people about what the Bible said and use that to talk about Aboriginal health and education. I liked his style. He was asking for better things for Aboriginal people, but he didn't want to put anybody offside. Later he was Sir Doug Nicholls and Governor of South Australia.

I thought maybe I could go up north and be a pastor like him. I'd done a part-time Bible course with the idea that some day I'd do missionary work with Aboriginal people. It didn't work out that way, but one time, when the missionary at Oodnadatta went on six weeks holiday, me and Lucy went up there to look after the kids at the mission. And it gave me the chance to see my parents and my brother when they came over from Mimili. I didn't really teach the Bible, but we had a little service on Sunday and Aboriginal people living near the mission would come over, and we'd sing the church hymns and all that.

When we got back to Adelaide, I decided to join the South Australian Branch of the Aboriginal Advancement League. Pastor Doug Nicholls was in the federal body. There were other Aboriginal people in the Advancement League, but I think the majority of the members were white people. It was the late 1960s and I knew things were happening. One Aboriginal man who came from the Alice Springs area was Charles Perkins, and he had been organising what they called the Freedom Bus Rides in the eastern states. I used to listen to him on the radio and he started to influence my thinking. I'd follow what he was doing: when he got his Bachelor of Arts degree from the university; all the trouble with the police during the Freedom Bus Rides; what he was saying about Aboriginal rights. And I went to hear him speak when he was in Adelaide. He talked about the need for better Aboriginal education, and health, and helping people with their own businesses. He talked about Aboriginal people needing the opportunity to be able to do things. And I thought: "Yeah, he's right on." Then I'd go and hear other Aboriginal people talk, like Margaret Valadian, and I could see she was a conservative.

My life sort of changed because of Charles Perkins. He really started me off. I thought a lot about what he was saying and I agreed with him. I wanted do some of the things he was doing. I'd look at the people at my church, and I could see that they were all conservatives. They were Christians all right, but they voted for the Liberal Party, just as I used to. I still liked Pastor Doug Nicholls' style, but listening to the things he said I could see he was right in with the conservative parties too. I knew I couldn't work for Aboriginal people properly if I stayed with the Church of Christ mob. I'd go to meetings of the Aboriginal Advancement League and tell them they weren't doing enough. Looked to me like they were mainly interested in welfare and raising money for things like Wiltja Hostel. They weren't doing enough outside of that. They weren't really interested in big changes in things like education and health for Aboriginal people. So I'd come out and talk like that, and they would sort of remind me, "Look, we don't want any Black Power here." They used to tell me off like that.

Anyway, I sent a tape to Jim Downing, saying: "Look, I'm interested in interpreting. Anything like that as long as I can get away from the Blind Institute." That place was really eating me. I would have stayed in Adelaide, if I could get other work. All my friends were there, from church and from work. But there just wasn't much. It must've been twelve months later when Jim Downing finally answered my tape: "You really interested?" I called him up and said: "My word. Never mind about the pay, I just want to go." At this time we had two children, Leroy and Rosemary. So Jim Downing talked to his bosses in the Congregational Church. They interviewed me and said: "All right. We'll give you twelve months' trial." I was feeling pretty good.

So I got a leave of absence from the Blind Institute. All my mates there said: "You'd be mad if you come back here! Go and stay away. This is just a mad house!" I knew I had my opportunity and I wasn't going to miss it. On 14 April 1970 we went to Alice Springs. And I've still kept a lot of my friends in Adelaide since then, but, for me, I made the right decision.

minakatingu – hands up

Alice Springs

So there we were, on a plane to Alice Springs. I'm married to lovely Lucy and we've got two kids: Leroy, born in 1967, and Rosemary, just eight weeks old. Nineteen-seventy model, that one. All the friends we'd made over the years in Adelaide came to the airport to say goodbye. I was sad, but I was happy too. After nearly fourteen years I'd finally left the Institute for the Blind for new work, and maybe a new life. A broomologist and his family.

Lucy'd been to Alice Springs before, but I didn't know what to expect. I've never seen Alice Springs. It was different from Adelaide: different smell, different air, and it was warm. When we got out of the plane, Reverend Jim Downing was waiting for us on the tarmac with his daughter, Kathy. Tjilpi Downing welcomed us there, and took us to where we were going to live.

He showed us this little house, a cottage, he called it. He said it was only temporary. There was just one big room with a bathroom and toilet. It turned out it was almost too cool inside at night. It was pretty basic, but it was all right, good enough for Anangu. So we sat down, and he starts to talk. We were pretty tired. The night before, Lucy worked hard packing things and getting ready and looking after Rosemary. Leroy had been crying during the night, and I had been up with him. I was trying to tell Tjilpi Downing that we needed some sleep, but when he starts talking, he can talk, that man! So me and Lucy were sitting there, and to him it looked like I was listening, but I was asleep. I don't think he noticed, because I keep my eyes shut most of the time anyway. When he finally left, Lucy said to me: "You know, when he was talking, I could hear you snoring a little bit."

Our house was near the Todd River, by the Old Timers Rest

Home. There were a lot of Ernabella people, Pitjantjatjara people, camped close by. The home was run by the Australian Inland Mission, it was really for aged people. But because the Uniting Church didn't have anywhere else, they negotiated the cottage for us.

I didn't start work straight away. In that first week, Tjilpi Downing said I couldn't do much. He told me, "Just take it easy and sort of get to know people." I think he was still working out how he was going to use me. He took me to his office. It wasn't much: there was a telephone and desk, just a little room with books and papers everywhere. It was the back part of what they called the Opportunity Shop. Once a week women from the church would come and get second-hand clothes out from the boxes, hang them out, and sell them to Aboriginal people. It was a good little shop. I bought a lot of shirts from that place. I think the church made some money from selling those clothes, and maybe half went for Aboriginal work.

We went around to meet the people Tjilpi Downing knew in town: doctors and sisters at the hospital, the police superintendent, social workers, and other people working at Native Welfare. And we saw Bernie Kilgariff, who was the chairperson of the Housing Commission board then. I'd say hello and talk a little bit. I could see this was going to be different: I'd come out in a different role. I was going to play a different part. I wasn't sure about it then, but I thought, "If I do a real good job, they might let me stay on after twelve months." I was already worrying that I might have to go back to Adelaide.

But it was slow at first. I think it was pretty hard for Jim Downing, and for me too. Oh, there was enough for me to do when I wasn't interpreting, but he was having trouble working it out. Lucy was at home, with the little ones, and I was meeting people all right, but I wanted to start.

Anyway, he had this little bit of office in the back room cleaned up, and he told me I'd be working there. He was going to do his work from his house. A lot of Anangu and other people came to see him there looking for help. The telephone at the office went to his place, and I was to take phone calls. It was always busy. But I didn't know how I was going to do interpreting. I was hidden there in the back where nobody could find me.

Then Tjilpi Downing started bringing Aboriginal people to me, or he'd send them down to the office. He'd talk to them and say: "Oh, *palya*, *tjilpi*. All right. You go down to that young fella. He'll help you." I'd see them and find out what they wanted. Most of the time they'd say they came in from somewhere in the bush: maybe Amata or Ernabella. Some came in from a new community set up by Native Affairs in the Petermann Ranges west of Ayers Rock called Docker River (a lot of people went to live there after spending years and years at Areyonga, a settlement on Western Arrernte land). They were mostly Pitjantjatjara and other people from the same language group, such as Ngaanyatjarra and Luritja. And they had no food and no money: "*Mai wiya*, money *wiya*." That's the first time I heard that, and I'm still hearing it today. Tjilpi Downing explained to me that when Anangu come out of the hospital – maybe they were there for X-rays or to see a specialist – they wouldn't have anything to eat with them, and I'd have to take them around the corner to Welfare. It was easy to get there from where I was working. I'd follow the fence along Hartley Street, tapping along with my white stick, with these Anangu following behind. I suppose it must have looked weird to them. Usually, if there's a blind person in the camp, they just sit there doing nothing, waiting to be fed, that's all. But this blind fella was trying to do something, but he couldn't see what he was doing.

I could still write Braille then, and Lucy helped me out with Pitjantjatjara spelling. I used to get people's names and write them out, you know, dot-dot-dot. I'd feel the paper with my fingers and read their names. I know those Anangu must've been thinking: "Hey. What's going on? What's he doing?" Then they'd go with me to Welfare to get what they called food vouchers. I'd have my paper with me, go in the office, and I'd read out the names. They'd ask me, "Are these people out there now?" I didn't know, of course, but I'd say yeah. Then they'd go out and make sure. I reckon they didn't trust me. Then they'd give me a whole lot of papers, and we'd go back. I'd hand them out and say: "Now, this is for food, not for other things. You can't get clothes and other things with this." I think Welfare had an agreement with Egar's Supermarket then. So I'd send them there, and they'd go to this special place in the back of Egar's, and the people working there would give them food in boxes – you know, meat, tea and sugar.

In Alice Springs at that time there were no organisations run by Aboriginal people. Anangu that I was helping out – Pitjantjatjara and Luritja people – were looked after by the three churches that were later to become the Uniting Church. One of these churches was the Congregational Church, and it had sent Jim Downing. Most of his work was with Anangu. The senior minister, from the Presbyterian Church, was Doug McKenzie. And the Methodist bloke was this young fella – fiery, red-headed, wild fella – called Ross Lane. Ross had a lot of new ideas: about how I should work and how to get white people educated about Anangu.

There were other churches too, for other Aboriginal people in town and in the bush. The Lutherans ran the Finke River Mission for Western Arrernte people. Eastern Arrernte people were looked after by the Catholic Church. The Baptist Church took care of the Warlpiri. They draft them out, like cattle, I suppose. And I knew all about that!

One idea that the Uniting Church had – it came from Jim Downing – was to start what they called the Institute for Aboriginal Development. The first stage of the IAD was built near the Methodist building in Bath Street, behind my office. Some of the money for the new IAD building came from the Federal Government. The Prime Minister then was Harold Holt. He made Billy Wentworth the first Minister for the Office of Aboriginal Affairs, and he gave the Uniting Church $14,000. The Harold Blair Foundation chucked in some money, but the church paid for most of it from donations made by members all over Australia.

At first I was paid by the Congregational Church, from a special Aboriginal fund, as welfare worker and interpreter. Later

I was a consultant to the IAD too. The church would sometimes take a special offering at the churches in Adelaide to help in the work I was doing. I was quite happy, anyway. I suppose I wanted to get paid, but I didn't care how much I got. I just wanted to do what I was doing. It was challenging for me to try and help Anangu. It was really good.

But I found out that Pitjantjatjara people are funny, they're funny people to work for. I was there to help any Anangu that came to me. As long as I could communicate, I'd try and help. That was my thinking, and that's what I did. But those Ernabella people would really get jealous and tell Lucy, "Yami should help only Ernabella people, nobody else." She'd tell me that, but it didn't change me. I kept doing my work and, after a time, they gave up their idea.

When Jim Downing thought more about what I should do, he organised for me to work in the Alice Springs courthouse every Monday. I used to get the list of Anangu that were going to get called up before the magistrate, and Jim's secretary would come and sit with me. I remember one morning there were one hundred and thirty names called out. There was always a bigger mob when the rodeo was on, or show weekends. Mainly they were charged for being drunk in a public place, using obscene words, things like that. There weren't many white people in court for those things. They had their own pubs, where they would drink. Anangu would buy their grog and go outside and drink in the park or in the street and get into trouble. There were no public facilities, except for one toilet and a cold water shower behind the Flynn Church. Nobody had a lawyer. There was no Aboriginal Legal Aid then. So when they were called up, they'd all plead guilty. Sometimes the magistrate would fine them. If it was a first offence, he'd let them go and say, "Don't let me see you again."

The only time I would interpret in the court was if somebody pleaded not guilty. Then the court would organise for a lawyer from one of the two firms in town. It didn't happen very often. I remember one day there was this bloke charged with something – I can't remember what it was – but he knew he wasn't guilty. I was talking to him and he said he wasn't going to plead not guilty because they would make him stay around and he wanted to go back where he came from. He told me if he said guilty, they'd let him go, then he'd see Pastor Albrecht, the Lutheran Minister, and tell him he didn't do it. Well, that was his thinking, just like a lot of Anangu I found out. He knew the church couldn't pay the fine – if they started doing that, they'd go broke – so he thought he could get a job or get somebody else to help.

I got to know the magistrates and the lawyers, and after a while I was doing quite a bit of interpreting. Not just in the court, but at the police station and in the hospital too. And I started to travel with Jim Downing out bush, and I'd interpret at the meetings. I worked pretty close with Tjilpi Downing. And he didn't just help Anangu. He'd go and visit anybody, white and black, in the hospital or anywhere. And a lot of people came to his house wanting help – a lot of Aboriginal people and different people, like new Australians from other countries. He'd help anybody, and they all knew him. Sometimes he'd go out bush and forget that he made an appointment. So they used to come to my office and I'd see them. They'd tell me their problem and I'd say: "Oh, all right. Well this one you can do." Or I might say, "On this one I think it'd be better if you ring Jim Downing when he comes back." I used to cover for him, you know, like a secretary. Apologise and all that. When Jim got back, he'd say: "Oh, good on you, *tjuu*. Sorry 'bout that, I forgot to tell you." I was learning by myself. If I didn't know, he'd help me. It was like that.

We talked a lot about the court. All right, I was helping out interpreting, and I did that for five years, but it wasn't enough. When I'd bring in the court lists to Tjilpi Downing he'd say: "It's pretty sad, Jim. This is sad. There's gotta be Aboriginal Legal Aid here." One day, a couple of years after I started working in Alice Springs, he said to me: "Look, they're having a big conference in Sydney. Judges, lawyers, barristers are going to be there. I want you to do a paper and go to that conference." Do a paper? I'd never done a paper before. I'm a broomologist, remember? And a stockman becoming an interpreter. I'm into work with my hands. I'm not a politician.

So I had to sit down and talk on a tape-recorder. Put down my ideas on Aboriginal people in the courts for all those lawyers. The conference was called "Aborigines, Human Rights and the Law". So I went to Sydney. There was a lot of people there: important judges and lawyers, and a lot of eastern Aboriginal people. So I went up and gave my little talk. I called it "Aborigines in the Court". I talked about Alice Springs, and Anangu getting into trouble with the police and all those things. When I finished, I got really good applause, you know. Then afterwards, those important people were talking to Jim Downing and I was there listening. I met Gordon Briscoe. He'd been helping to start up Redfern Aboriginal Legal Service and we talked about that. And I saw Neville Perkins – Charles Perkins' nephew. He was learning law at the University of Sydney then. Through that, I think Tjilpi Downing invited those Redfern people to come up to Alice Springs.

They had a lot of meetings then. Tjilpi Downing was involved in that, and I went too, but I was very much in the background. That was all right. Then, I think in 1972 some time (not long before IAD moved to where it is today on South Terrace), Central Australian Aboriginal Legal Aid started. They had a little office around the corner from me, on Hartley Street. The first person to work there was an Arrernte fella by the name of Georgie Bray. Neville Perkins was around then, and he used to see Jim Downing a lot and talk about Legal Aid. At first they didn't have lawyers, but then they started getting them from the south.

Another thing Tjilpi Downing was involved with then was setting up an Aboriginal medical service for Alice Springs. I think the idea came from Redfern again. On that one, I didn't go to the meetings, but there were a lot of other people there: Charles Perkins and a good friend of mine, Elliott McAdam. Anyway, about the same time as the legal service, the Central Australian Aboriginal Congress started. And both of them are still there in Alice Springs today.

117

When all this was going on, changes were happening at IAD. As I said, I worked as a consultant to IAD, and I had a lot to do with it in those early days. Jim Downing was there, of course, and so were a lot of good white people from the church. The IAD had three aims, or that's what it seemed to me – Jim Downing might have had others. One was to run the Mother and Babies Health Centre. They had a white sister come down from Yirrkala, in the Top End, to help set it up. She was a lovely woman and a missionary. Her name was Sister Lawton and she was with the mothers for twelve months. The second aim was Tjilpi Downing's idea. He thought it was very important to have language classes, so doctors, nurses, welfare workers, and police could learn some Aboriginal language. I took that over from Jim, along with Nyiinga Stewart and his wife. The third aim was community development, and that's what Jim Downing was doing.

There was a fourth one, but it didn't last long, and that was for Anangu to learn proper English pronunciation. Jim Downing got this black woman from America to give us lessons. I think her husband worked at Pine Gap. She'd teach us at the Old Timers Home: me and Stanley Douglas and this other fella called Sid somebody. So we'd learn how to say pie, buy, shop, shoe, and all those different sounds. And there was this old whitefella at Old Timers then: proper *tjilpi* and a nice old fella – he would've been close to sixty. He used to bring the two other blokes to classes. And he'd come up to me and tease me; make out he's talking an Aboriginal language and say, "Blah blah blah blah…" Used to make me laugh. But when he saw who was teaching us, saying shoes and shops and all that, he said, "Hey, I wanna come learn English too." She was very beautiful.

Then the Uniting Church decided that the IAD had to be separate from the church, so it could receive government funding for Aboriginal work. They got one of their members to come up from Canberra. He was an administrator, and he was going to set up a system for the IAD – the way it was going to work – incorporate it, get a board of directors, and so on. The Uniting Church put five people on the board, and there had to be at least four Aboriginal people, and the rest came from organisations in town. So, one board member was from the hospital, and another was the manager of the Commonwealth Bank. I never knew what that was for. It was always an aim of the Uniting Church, and it was in the constitution, that one day the IAD would be handed over fully to Aboriginal control. And later on it was.

The first chairperson was Dr Kerry Kirk, and Jim Downing was the director. They bought a block of land on South Terrace, along the Todd River. But there was no building for the IAD, just an old hostel that they decided to keep for Aboriginal people from the bush who needed to stay in town.

Jim Downing got this idea. Because he was a church minister, one job he had was to visit everybody, you know, visit his flock inside the Uniting Church boundary. I think he went over the fence sometimes, just for his own interest, going to places like Hermannsburg, Areyonga, Yayi Yayi and Papunya. Anyway, he'd go down to Finke, along the Ghan railway line, as part of his Uniting Church work. One time he was watching these Finke people telling a story to some little kids and drawing a horseshoe shape in the dirt to give the idea of a windbreak or *kanku*, that old-time house made of sticks and spinifex. Jim Downing started to think that maybe the IAD building could be like that. In the middle there'd be a courtyard with trees, where people would sit down and take a course. So when he got back to town, he got an architect to draw up his idea. And that's how the IAD got that funny-shaped building. When Anangu would come in from the street, they used to comment on it: "*Ngangkarpa*. Hey. This is a lovely-looking *kanku*."

The IAD moved into its new building in 1973. Because Jim Downing was director, the church decided he would have to work for the IAD full-time. I was still doing consultant work, and the board – which was mostly church people anyway – put me on full-time too. Altogether, with office workers and some others, there were about ten people working at the IAD then.

Besides IAD, the Uniting Church was involved in two other things: doing spiritual work with its members and running what

119

they called the Cross-Culture Group. I was really interested in the Cross-Culture Group and I became chairperson for three years. There was mostly white people in it – maybe forty or fifty of them – and they didn't just come from the Uniting Church. We picked them up from the workplace – a lot from the hospital and from welfare. There were Catholics and Lutherans, mostly women, and there were a lot of Americans. It didn't have a constitution, but its main thing was race relations: how to mix black and white together. When I thought about Charles Perkins' Freedom Bus Rides and Sir Doug Nicholls' message about working in with white people, I knew Aboriginal people couldn't solve the problems themselves. White and black had to live and work together. They had to learn how to accept each other. Without that, Alice Springs would be a racist town. It is sad, but that's what it has become.

There were Pitjantjatjara people in the Cross-Culture Group, and we tried to get different Aboriginal people to come too, the Arrernte and Warlpiri. But it didn't work. We knew – Pitjantjatjara people knew – that Alice Springs was on Arrernte land, and that's why we wanted to involve Arrernte people with us. I would talk to Anangu I knew about that, and they'd say: "Oh, that's right. This is their country, those Arrernte. We just come here because it's a whitefella town. The whitefella took the land from the Arrernte, but the town's here now, gotta be here." We kept trying to get Arrernte people into the IAD, but it was hard. It wasn't until later that they came up with another idea. I'll get back to that.

It was a good organisation the Cross-Culture Group. Every month we'd have a meeting and sometimes show pictures in the IAD theatre room. If any visitors were coming through – they might be Maori, or people from New Guinea – we asked them to come and give a talk and put on their food. One Maori fella, I remember, put on a deadly show, cooking this meat in what he called a *hangi*. Beautiful. And sometimes we'd have a picnic, and some Anangu would show people in the group all the bush tucker. We'd tell stories, eat chops and sausages, and have a good time.

Race problems were getting pretty bad in Alice Springs in the early 1970s. In the newspapers, white people were rubbishing what they called "blackfellas". Nothing new, same thing happens today. But it was new to me then. Talking about drunken Aborigines; talking about white people walking on one side of the street and blackfellas on the other side; policemen rough-handling blackfellas. And no one was around to say anything against it. Jim Downing was still there, fighting, and I used to say to him, "Look, the church should be coming out and answering this."

As the chairperson of the Cross-Culture Group, I had to think of something. I called a meeting and said: "Righto, we gotta take it head on. We gotta face up to these people. But how to do it, what do we do?" They had an idea. They said to get these people, you got to get them in one place, in a room, and talk things out. And invite the top people: police commissioner, town mayor, all the important people. There was an organisa-tion called Australian Frontier, and it was based in Canberra. They had experts that could organise a meeting like that – they called it community consultation – and they'd get everybody to talk, just bring everything out. Some people might be rude, but they would let them talk. They'd ask a lot of questions and get them thinking, help them work their problems out, or try to find out if something else was worrying them. It sounded good, but we didn't have much money. So we sold cakes and things to raise funds and get these people to come.

We organised it, and it happened. Got everybody in the theatre room at the IAD, and they went for it. And that bloke from the Frontier Service, he just loved it. He got them to come out with their true feelings – no bullshit. The police would get real cranky, but we'd say they were important and we wanted their help. We'd give them ways to ease the problems and things like that. We'd ask them why is it that policemen always pick up Aboriginal people and leave the whitefellas? You go to the Monday morning court and it's always blackfellas. Why is that? All those kind of things we'd ask. And some of the white people would come out and really say what they were thinking. They were really angry and wild about something. I found it very interesting, but very frightening. Later on the Cross-Culture Group did a similar thing, but without the Frontier Service.

It wasn't easy for Aboriginal people to live in Alice Springs, or even to visit there. When I came in 1970, people from the bush would camp where they could, close to town or near the Todd River. There were no water taps, no firewood, and no shelters. The Uniting Church had a small hostel for Pitjantjatjara people, but it wasn't enough, and it didn't help the Arrernte people from the Alice Springs area at all.

There was one place called Amoonguna, a community about eight miles out of town run by Native Affairs. Arrernte people lived there – it was their country, of course – and it was where people were supposed to stay when they came into town. So they had all these Aboriginal people from different places there, and they'd always be telling me it was just too much trouble. Fights and arguments all the time. When people used to come in from Docker River, they'd be taken to Amoonguna by Welfare. But all the time they'd get out and camp in the creek down from Old Timers. I used to visit them and get food for them. Welfare used to tell me: "Look, we put them at Amoonguna where they have a community kitchen. It's not our fault if they're hungry." I used to have quite an argument about that. I'd say: "Can't they have choices? People should be allowed to live where they want to, and Welfare should provide things for them." It was hard then, talking to Welfare and Native Affairs people.

The Cross-Culture Group started by trying to get a living area for Anangu coming into town for their own business, for medical reasons, or maybe for shopping. We took people around looking for a place on the east side of town, near Spencer Hill and in the Sadadeen area. We wrote to the Northern Territory Administrator about the problems of Aboriginal people living in Alice Springs and the need for some land for them. We were told that we could have twenty acres in Alice Springs, just through the Gap near Little Sisters camp. That was good of them, but they said it was to cater for everybody. And we knew it wasn't going to work with different Aboriginal people living there together.

Pitjantjatjara people weren't happy to just live there without asking the Arrernte first. They told me it was my job to go and talk to the Lutheran pastor at the Finke River Mission – that's the Western Arrernte church. I did that and the Arrernte agreed for the Pitjantjatjara people to have that land. The Cross-Culture Group put up two ablution blocks and a laundry at Little Sisters and I remember Danny Colson built the fence around the camp. Pitjantjatjara and Luritja people went to live there, and people who used to camp near Old Timers just stayed there.

Getting a place for Pitjantjatjara people visiting Alice Springs helped stop the trouble at places like Amoonguna, but it didn't help the Arrernte trying to live in town on their own country. As I said, they weren't happy about getting mixed up with the Cross-Culture Group or the IAD then. I could see they needed to have their own organisation.

At this time, I was travelling around to the hospital and court and everywhere on behalf of IAD with this young fella from Adelaide called Elliott McAdam. He was studying with the Aboriginal Task Force and he'd come up to Alice Springs for on-the-job training. He was really good eyes for me, and we became good friends. We heard about this other Aboriginal bloke, just come back from his second time in Vietnam. His name was Geoff Shaw. We went to ask him to come to the Cross-Culture Group.

At first he said, "*Wiya*. No way. I'm a soldier." He could talk a little bit of Luritja. Then I told him: "No, you gotta job to do. Look. In this town, there's Anangu coming in all the time. Might be Ti-Tree way, or Tennant Creek or from your communities. Which way you from anyway?"

"I'm a Kaytetye."

"All right. Good. I'm a Yankunytjatjara. You know what's going on here. There are people coming into Alice Springs and there's nothing for them. And you're going to do something about it. We're gonna find a living place for them. We're gonna find water taps for them. We're gonna get firewood for them. Like that."

"*Wiya, wanti.* Leave me alone." But we kept talking and then he started coming around: "All right. If I'm gonna do that I can't do it from the Cross-Culture Group."

"OK. Whaddya want?"

"I want to have our own group. That's one language group."

"OK. We'll help you to start." I said: "Jim Downing's good at that. He can help you to start off."

So he got the Arrernte people together and they had their first meeting in the IAD theatre room. Jim Downing was there and I was in the background. They said: "Right. Institute for Aboriginal Development does education and training. We gotta start for town-lease camps. We gotta work for Arrernte people living in town." They knew the Town Council wouldn't help. We used to talk to them through the Cross-Culture Group, but they'd just say that too many blackfellas were camping around the town area. They should be through the Gap or they should be at Amoonguna, they said. The Town Council and some other important whitefellas just didn't want to see Aboriginal people in town. It hasn't really changed that much: they still talk about "cleaning up the Todd River".

Back then, a lot of Aboriginal people were leaving the stations, out of work, and wanting to make Alice Springs their base. There were nine or ten town camps, where people were just sitting down. Arrernte people at that first meeting decided to start with them: putting in water taps, tents, getting firewood. Later, they would try to get proper leases from the Northern Territory Government. They came up with the name Tangentyere Council. Later on, Jim Downing got a lawyer, Peter Tiffen, and he worked for free, helping to draw up the constitution and setting up the organisation. So that's where Tangentyere Council started: at the IAD.

Around this time, Jim Downing asked me to go to a conference at Monash University in Melbourne. He wanted me to do another paper, this time on health. I worked on it with a tape-recorder as I had done before and called it "Between Black and

White". Funny he asked me to talk about health, because mine wasn't very good then. There was something wrong: I was coughing a lot, bringing up vomit, and I couldn't breathe properly. I'd gone to our family doctor, Barry Wittenbury, a good doctor and a really down-to-earth man. He checked me over and said he could see some bastard was in there making me sick, but the bloody X-rays just wouldn't show him what it was. If I was going to Melbourne, he could send me to a specialist.

It was a big conference: doctors everywhere. People from Western Australia, Queensland, all over. After I gave my paper, and they asked questions, I felt that it was too much for me to take in. I could see Tjilpi Downing talking to all the big fellas. Then I met a young doctor, just got back from New Guinea. His name was Trevor Cutter, and I said to him: "Hey, you wanna come to Central Australia? There's a new Aboriginal medical service just starting. Just new and you'd find it interesting." I talked to him about how I was feeling too, and he organised for me to see this specialist. He drove me to Bethlehem Hospital for more X-rays. And all the time I was telling him about Alice Springs.

As everyone knows, Trevor Cutter came up to Alice Springs and was there for a long time. I think it was one of the best things we did. He was the backbone of Congress, good with people, and we learnt a lot from him. He was just a young man when he passed away, and it was very sad to see him go.

They found out I had pneumonia in the bottom of one of my lungs. I went to the hospital in Melbourne and they put a tube down my throat to drain it out. I didn't want to stay there, so Trevor Cutter arranged through the specialist and Dr Wittenbury for me to go back to Alice Springs for treatment. After the conference, Jim Downing gave me three weeks off. I went to the physiotherapist every day and he cleared my lungs right out.

There was another important thing happening in the early 1970s, when I was at IAD. I had heard about these people called the Gurindji, and how in August 1966 they walked off Wave Hill Station and went to Wattie Creek. I know there were other times when Aboriginal people in places like Western Australia had walked off the stations before that. But I think that the beginning of what everybody started calling "land rights" happened with the Gurindji. There was a mining company, called Nabalco, that wanted to dig for bauxite in the Gove Peninsula. Aboriginal people living there had been given twenty-eight days to object in the *Government Gazette*. They didn't see it, of course, but Gordon Bryant, Federal Labor Party member, did, and when he got to Darwin he helped some of the people there write an objection. That was the start of the first land rights case. I didn't really understand what was going on, but I'd talk to a friend of mine about it, a social worker by the name of Colin Clague. When Justice Blackburn handed down his judgment, and it went against the Aboriginal traditional owners, I reckon that's when all Aboriginal people became strong. It was a turning point, and from then they moved forward on land rights.

The churches were sympathetic. The Uniting Church, Catholics, and Anglicans – I never heard about the Baptists or Lutherans or my old church, the Church of Christ – were openly supporting Aboriginal people on the question of land rights. I knew there was a big movement happening, especially in the southern states. South Australia probably had the first land rights law and that started up the Aboriginal Land Trust. It wasn't really an Aboriginal organisation because its executive was appointed by the Minister. It could hold land, but only Aboriginal reserves. But it was a start. There was another organisation that came after the 1967 Referendum. I think it was called the Council for Aboriginal Affairs. Dr Nugget Coombs was the chairman; Charles Perkins, Margaret Laurie and Reg Saunders were on it too. In 1972 Dr Coombs got the money to buy Everard Park Station (Mimili). Then around the same time, the Labor Government of Gough Whitlam appointed Judge Woodward to look into land rights in the Northern Territory. I remember they came to Alice Springs, and I interpreted for them at Docker River.

It started to change my thinking. I still felt that Aboriginal people needed education and health and welfare. But to have these things, they needed to have their own land. Tribal people – the Pitjantjatjara, Luritja, and Pintupi – lived away from the towns. They were thinking they could run their own organisations, their own health clinics, their own businesses. And to do that they needed their own land, not somebody else's. Anangu knew that it was their land all the time. The boundaries came with the white people. The *malu* and *ngintaka wapar* was still there, and all the others. It was our *waparitja*. That's what really changed me.

I worked for the IAD until 1975. When I left, I asked Dr Trevor Cutter to take over as chairperson of the Cross-Culture Group. He was interested, but he was busy with his medical work. A lot of things were never followed up. Four years later, nothing much had been done and we didn't know where the members had gone. There was still money in the bank that we used for making press statements, for our social activities, and for helping Anangu catch the train or the bus, or to buy food and blankets. I decided to start the Group up again, just for a while. I went and talked to Geoff Shaw at Tangentyere Council and arranged to have the twenty acres at Little Sisters and what money there was in the bank given over to Tangentyere. I don't know who owns that land today – I think maybe Congress holds the lease. There's still a town camp there, and it's also used by Pitjantjatjara Council, Tangentyere and the Central Australian Aboriginal Media Association.

Anyway, in the end, the Cross-Culture Group just died. I'm sorry to say that. It was just volunteers that made it up, but we did a lot of things together. We all enjoyed working with people, black and white. Even the kids were involved. It was a good group, and I still miss it today.

Back to Mimili

I had a new job and it was going to be the hardest one for me yet. I was back at Mimili, old Everard Park, this time with my own family. We drove down from Alice Springs in our Holden ute and just moved into the homestead – near the old one, where my boss the Ponder Brothers and David Joseland used to live; where I used to pinch lemons; where I used to work in the garden with old Mitchelburk. I'd left more than twenty years before as a jackeroo, and now I was back as the manager of the station.

It wasn't owned by whitefellas any more. As I said, the Government bought the Everard Park pastoral lease on behalf of the Mimili people three years before, in 1972. The station was like a lot of the others that the Aboriginal Loan Fund Commission was buying all over Australia: mainly broken-down properties with worn-out windmills, rusty tanks, stockyards nearly falling over. The white pastoralists had usually got their money's worth, and they wanted to get out. David Joseland, the previous owner of Everard Park, had another good reason to be happy he sold the lease: there'd been a drought all around for eleven years. I'd heard from one of the new managers of Mimili that it rained forty inches in the next twelve months after Joseland left. He also said that the rains brought so many mice and rats they nearly overran the place.

Along with the cattle station was the Mimili community, and about one hundred and thirty-five people, mostly Yankunytjatjara, lived there. They were mainly my relations, of course. My mother and Kanytji were still at Mimili, and so was my brother, Shannon, and his family. I first went back with Sister Dot Forbes, when everybody was living at Bettys Well, and I used to visit them when I worked in Alice Springs.

The Mimili Cattle Company started up after the Joseland family left, but it employed only about six or seven men, so most people were getting pensions or unemployment benefits. The community paid for one bore and they put a little three-thousand-litre tank on top of a hill near the camp. They also got a Bedford truck and water trailer, and the pensioners and workers would chuck in for spare parts. There were no houses and no school. The cattle company had a little store selling tea, flour, sugar — just basic food. If people wanted something a bit flash, they'd go to Indulkana or Fregon. Dr Trevor Cutter used to come through on medical patrol in a van from Central Australian Aboriginal Congress in Alice Springs.

So the Aboriginal people got the land back — they had the station anyway — except they didn't manage it themselves. When the Government bought Mimili, the Department of Aboriginal Affairs got this consultancy firm to run the cattle business. The community would have to look after itself. The consultancy firm was the same outfit that advised the Government on what properties were good to buy: were they money-making concerns, commercially viable, and all that stuff. They tried two managers at Mimili, but both times they didn't work out with the local people. I heard they were very good with cattle: they understood cattle work, management of the place, trucking, marketing, bookkeeping, fences, and all that. There was only one thing they didn't understand: Aboriginal culture. They'd be in the stockyard working, and one of the managers would say something that offended one of the Aboriginal men — a tribal man doing stock work. Or he'd make a rude comment to the young men in front of *tjitji*, you know, kids. There was a lot of problems or misunderstandings like that. Anangu would tell Jim Downing that the manager had to change his ways. And Jim Downing always talked to Dr Coombs in Canberra. I suppose those managers could've gone and done Aboriginal culture and language training so they might understand people better. But that didn't happen and it didn't work out.

After the second manager went, the Department of Aboriginal Affairs said to Mimili people: "OK. We're sick of you mob. Pick your own manager." And they did. They picked me – the blind man. DAA was not happy. "If you're gonna do that, you can do it on your own. Make your own money. We're not going to help you." And they took all their support away, because they didn't like me going there.

They still asked me if I wanted the job. I was working at the IAD, and I thought the best way for me to go to Mimili was on secondment from IAD. I could help out, at least until they found somebody else. Lucy said she would support me. St Philips College in Alice Springs agreed that Leroy could go to school there, and Lucy would give Rosie a bit of schooling in the first twelve months at Mimili. Our new daughter, Karina, was just a baby. It was going to be hard for a blind man, but I wanted to take on the bastard. Only this time, to look at me, I was going to need a bigger horse and a bigger saddle!

So there we were. It didn't take long to work out that the cattle company didn't have much, and the community had even less. We knew we could get help from some people living at Mimili. Teddy Brown was there, and his wife – she's passed away now – was doing some of the bookkeeping, but they left soon after we arrived, so the only person who could read and write was Lucy. She worked flat out for no pay all the time we were there: running the station store, helping the pensioners, doing the books, getting out the wages and social benefits cheques. And she was looking after our kids. She's a great worker and she supported me all the way. For the cattle company, Sammy Dodd was keeping the bores running. There were a few stockmen: uncle Harry Wallatina, Andy Dega, Willy, and my brother, Shannon. Ringo was in the workshop.

Then I met the accountant from Alice Springs. So, right. "Now, Mr Lester, Mimili Cattle Company owes…" I think it was $110,000 for windmills, tanks and bores; $25,000 to the auditors in Adelaide; $10,000 backpay to the stockmen; and over $100,000 in equipment and feed. It turned out that one of our creditors, Elders GM, was very good to Mimili Cattle Company. They carried us all the way. And one other good thing: we had cattle and horses, but I didn't know how many.

The Lands Department allowed forty-five hundred head, and there were at least that many.

I called a meeting of the Mimili Council. They were the boss now, and it was my job, as manager, to talk to them. I said: "Look. Mimili is your place now. You used to work for the whitefella owner, and you did that work well for him. He trucked his cattle to the market, got the money for them and paid everything he had to. That's how he kept going. This time you gonna do the same work, only difference is – it's yours. It's your place, your horses, your cattle. You people can call me manager, and that's all right. But I'm not really like the old-time manager: what I call myself is an organiser. And I'm gonna organise you people to do certain jobs. And we'll beat this DAA for leaving us and saying we gotta make our own money."

So we got down to it. Mimili Cattle Company had one old, tray-top Land Rover, a broken-down Toyota tray-top, stock-camp trailer, and bits and pieces. The tucker box from the trailer was at Bettys Well; the twelve-gallon water drum was at Cork-wood Bore; and the trailer was at Ronalds Bore, with no tyres. I said: "We've gotta put all that together for the stock camp. Which vehicle used to tow the trailer?" Land Rover. But it was sick, sitting down someplace. The Bedford truck was fucked – starter motor. I found out there was a Holden station wagon: it was finished. The only thing going was my Holden ute – just.

This was getting too hard. I asked them: "Who knows a little bit about mechanic work?"

Sammy Dodd said, "Oh, yeah. I know a little bit. And me and David Umala and Ringo know about fixing windmills too."

"Anybody else?"

Somebody said he could work on the windmills, but he'd leave the thinking to the others with the fixing know-how.

"OK. What about runnin' the stock camp?" There was a lot that knew about that.

They said, "Oh, yeah, we all can do that, but we leave it to Shannon." My younger brother. He looked like he was happy to do it, and they were happy to work with him.

"OK. Look," I said. "Things are gonna be tough. You gonna

work like in old days. But Mimili Cattle Company will give you cigarettes, matches, and cigarette papers, and feed you. It's just for little while till things get better. Then you'll go on award wages and you'll get backpay. For now, we'll do some branding, and get fat bullocks for trucking. You'll get ten dollars a head for the bullocks, and one dollar for every calf branded. Just until things get better." And they agreed. *Palya.*

And that's how we worked. The first problem was to get water to the cattle. A lot of the bores needed repairing, and the rods and columns had to be pulled. To do that, we at least needed a four-wheel drive, and all we had was my old Holden ute. I wasn't going to let it beat us. I wasn't going begging to the whitefellas on my hands and knees. I said to Sammy Dodd, "Look, all the cars are broke down except this ute of mine. I remember on Granite Downs before I went blind, I seen Tommy Singer use a triple block with a little car like this one to pull the bores." And Sammy said, "Oh, yeah, yeah! I seen that too!" So we did that and managed to get water to the cattle during the hottest part of summer.

To get some money, we mustered a hundred head and trucked them down to Gepps Cross market. Next thing I heard was from our agent, wanting a cheque to pay the freight. The cattle had been sold for $30 a head, and that didn't even meet costs. We couldn't pay, of course, and so we asked Elders to carry us. And they did. That was my first time, my first go at the market. I would have to get better, so I decided to wait before we sold any more.

We were really stuck. I cut down to three stockmen, and I said to the others: "We gotta do it another way till things get better. Don't worry, it'll happen. One day." I went to my brothers – Andy Dega, Shannon, and Sammy Dodd – and asked them: "Hey, you seen any old wooden buggy wheels? You know, the ones with the iron tyre?"

"Oh, yeah, sure. Whaddya want it for?" I told them I wanted to stretch bullock hide. "Oh, that's right. That's what they did. We used to do it a long time ago, when Ponder brothers was here."

"That's him. We gotta go back to that."

"Ah, look *tjuu*, forget it. That's all finished now. When we worked for Mr Joseland, he got us R. M. Williams straps, cotton ropes, and nylon ropes."

"Yeah, well that was different. Mr Joseland, he had money. Mimili Cattle Company got fuck all. We gotta go back to the old way. This is what I learnt at Granite Downs and you did too."

I asked the men about the saddles. They said: "Oh, there's six saddles, fully mounted with stirrups, girth and everything." But the others had no bridles and maybe only one stirrup.

"Hey, we got one-legged cowboys round here!"

"*Wiya*, *tjuu*. Ah, some fellas must've took the stirrup straps away for a swag strap."

"Yeah? And what about the girth and surcingle?"

"Oh, the kids took those and cut them up for shanghais." Fuckin' *tjitji*!

Mimili Cattle Company might not've had much, but there was plenty to eat walking around. So when they got a killer for the station and for the community, I'd ask them to bring the fat – kidney fat and guts fat. I was doing like Tommy Singer: getting the oil from the fat. I'd be out there in the yard, boiling it up in two buckets I found. Putting in the kerosene and onion to make a nice smell. And I boiled up all the saddle cloths in a forty-four-gallon drum of water that Sammy Dodd cut in half for me. Scrubbed all fifteen of them with a brush. And little Rosemary would come out there and stay with me. *Mingkiri*, I used to call her – little mouse. She was helping me, she said.

When I had the fat ready in two flour drums – one clear, and one mixed with Stockholm tar – Sammy Dodd, Andy Dega, and Willy came around: "Hey, what's that for, brother? Looks like what they used in the old days. They don't have that any more, you know. Mr Joseland had proper stuff for sores on the horse. It was in a bottle. You'd shake it and mix it with water, and it's blue."

"Oh. Well, might be I'm colour blind. What's this one?"

"It's black!" And we'd all laugh and I'd say: "Look, this is olden time medicine." And when I used Tommy Singer's name,

133

they'd laugh some more. They remembered him, poor old thing.

I used to have a meeting with the Mimili Council every month and I'd tell them how we were going, saying we were up the creek mostly. We weren't killing often enough to make the hobble straps and ropes we needed. So I went and told them my idea about giving meat for doing work for the cattle company, and all of them said: "*Uwaaaa!* No worries. Why bother asking? *Kuka palya!*" They were lovely.

I went to Tjiḻpi Kanytji and his cousin. They both got sit-down money. I said to my uncle, "Hey, *tjiḻpi!* When you were at De Rose Hill Station, you used to do leather work, right? Making bridles and things like that? Well, what 'bout you helping me, 'cause Mimili Cattle Company got no money. Money *wiya*. This is your station, your cattle, you know. If you do leather work, the cattle company will give you meat, you know, *kuka*."

Everybody had to help. There were diesel engines – pump-jacks – at the bores to pump the water. I went to the old blokes: "*Wai*, can you help?" And they said: "Yeah, we'll go and sit down and start the engine. We can go for *kuka* or wood for boomerangs during the day. That's all right, *palya*." So I got Tjiḻpi William, my father's brother, at Bettys Well; Tjiḻpi Kanytji at Victory Well; and Tjiḻpi Pompey at Gap Well. All pumping water for the cattle.

When I got everybody working, I soon had enough bullock hides. But then I started worrying about how many killers we were eating. I went to Tjiḻpi Kanytji: "You know that bullock hide? Well, it's good for hobble straps, but we can't be eating the bullocks all the time. I remember long time ago, *tjiḻpi*, you used to make hobble straps for camels from rubber tyres. And for the camel ropes, you used to slice back the hemp rope and put a Turk's head knot on the other end. You still got the idea?"

"*Uwa, uwa.* I remember." So, next time I was in Alice Springs I went to Elders and got ordinary nylon ropes and rings. I brought them back to Tjiḻpi Kanytji and he used the big rings to make head ropes, and the small rings for leg ropes.

134

When they made all that, I took it to stock camp: nylon ropes, home-made bridles with copper rivets, hobble straps made from rubber tyres. I went up to Andy Dega, gave him the ropes and all the rest, and all the stockmen just pissed themselves laughing: "You can't use these hobbles, they're rubbish!"

"Look, they'll keep the horses. They won't go far."

"Wait a minute. Wait a minute, brother, just look at this. These hobbles are for camels!" Gee, they were funny fellas. But they used them.

We worked hard. And when things were getting a little better, I started thinking about the cattle we had, how to manage them. The Aboriginal Loan Fund Commission had just bought Kenmore Park, and Donald Fraser was running that with a board of directors of twelve Anangu from Ernabella. Me and Donald sort of helped each other all the time I was at Mimili. Kenmore had a truck and I was using it to shift bulls from one bore to the other – shifting them to a different mob of cows. All the men thought that was pretty funny.

Later on, when we got new Shorthorn bulls, we tried to yard the old ones to truck them out for market. But they were too big and too nasty. So we had to shoot them on the spot. They weren't interested in the cows anyway. I don't know why: maybe they were too old or too big.

One other thing I did. I had a little radio, and every midday, I used to listen to the ABC Country Hour. And they'd talk about the market: what the cattle price was doing. One time they said that prices were going up fourteen per cent next week. So I went to see Cassidy Uluru and my brother Shannon. We weren't doing much cattle work then: just checking the fences and keeping up the water. They were sitting down in the camp. We sent about eighty head to market. We got our first good price for them.

Then I started listening to station people talking to each other on their radios. The IAD had let me use a transceiver that I kept in my ute. So, after five o'clock, I'd go out and sit in the car – just listening. They didn't know I was there. One evening, this fella from Elders was asking: "Anybody got store cattle?

135

There's a lotta people lookin' for dry cows and mixed-sexed weaners." And I thought, "Hey, we've got some I think."

Next day I rang Elders on the radio telephone – cow of a thing. You'd waste all day waiting for that phone. I talked to the manager: "*Wai!* Is there a market for store cattle?" And he said: "No, no. Sorry mate, there's nothing."

"Oh, yeah." But I recognised his voice. I heard him talking on the radio to Kenmore, to the same white manager that was at Mimili before me and to McLachlan's manager at Granite Downs. But when I ring up, there's no market.

Later on, Southern Farmers called me and said: "Look, we're lookin' for bullocks."

And I told him, "I'm your man."

"Right. You'll have to truck to the railhead at Oodna."

"Look. I got 'em here. I can only sell onna place."

"Oh no. Just send 'em down. I'll come out and you truck 'em down to Gepps Cross."

"No, nothin' doin'," I said, "I gotta sell 'em onna place. I don't wanna pay freight."

"OK. Look, I'll come up and talk business."

"Sure. No worries."

We had sixty head at Robbs Well. I asked Tommy Dodd, Andy Dega and Shannon: "What are they like? Are they good?" And they said: "Fat. They're all fat bullocks." The agent from Southern Farmers come up, like he said, and had a look: "Well, hmmm. I'd really like it if you can truck 'em down and we'll sell 'em for you at the market."

"I don't want to sell it to the market. You take 'em or leave 'em. There it is. You pay for 'em in this yard or leave 'em. Doesn't matter to us." So he went over to his car and started talking to this other bloke sitting there. He comes back and says: "All right, I'll pay for 'em on the place." He arranged for a double-decker truck to come from Mt Willoughby and pick up the cattle, and he paid the money into the Mimili Cattle Company account. Elders must've seen the money in there; but we still had debts.

Southern Farmers came back. This time they wanted a full trainload. So we sold them eleven hundred and fifty-seven fat bullocks: eleven hundred dry cows and the rest were mixed-sex weaners. From that one, we paid all our bills. The manager from Elders rang me up: "Hey, what's this going on? We've been carrying you all this time and you made two truckings with Southern Farmers?" And I said: "Sorry, mate. I asked you if you had a store market and you told me you didn't."

"Oh. Right. Did you get a good price for them?"

"No worries," I said, "we're laughin'. After we pay what we owe you and Southern Cross, with the next lot we truck I'll be able to pay backpay to all our stockmen." And we did that. After eighteen months, we were in front.

Then the Department of Aboriginal Affairs came back and said: "Look, we've been watching you people. You're going well, now whaddya want?"

"It's not what I want," I said. "It's what community wants. Mimili Cattle Company and community should have a shared mechanic. The community should have funding like Ernabella and Indulkana. They should have a community adviser and the benefits of other communities. And Mimili Cattle Company should have a cattle consultant. Not to tell stockmen how to put saddles and hobbles on a horse, but how to get new bulls; advice on marketing and bookkeeping."

DAA agreed. They funded the new positions and they arranged for Aputula Housing to build a store and new houses at Mimili. To cut a long story short, in 1979 Mimili Cattle Company made a small profit. We had sixty-four new bulls and we'd bought forty-four new horses, unbroken and broken ones, from Victoria River Downs. I got a thoroughbred stallion and a heavy Arab-cross for new stock. And the seasons had been good, so there was plenty of feed. Nine men were in the stock camp, all on award wages. Mimili Cattle Company got them beautiful R. M. Williams leather straps, beautiful nylon rope, cotton head ropes, new saddle cloths and saddles. The stock-men were really happy. Sammy Dodd and his brother were full-time on the bore run; Ringo was trainee mechanic. Things were going good, so I said it was time for me to go. The other thing for me was that Jim Downing was taking twelve months' leave as IAD Director to write a book on Aboriginal homelands. The board asked me to come back to IAD to take over for that time. It was time for me to leave Mimili.

* * *

It had been raining for two days the morning we left, and it rained for a good part of that April. I wanted to leave. Cattle work always goes on, and anyway I thought I'd done as much as I could. Mimili Cattle Company had finally made a profit, and things were going good at the community. I had a new job at the IAD, and Leroy and Rosie had to be in Alice Springs for school. Still, it was hard leaving all those people there. We decided to go early because we didn't want to say goodbye to all our friends and relations – it was too sad. All right, we were only going to Alice Springs, but I was glad people didn't come out from their houses and *kanku* and Holden station wagons on that rainy morning.

So we just went. There was a lot of water on the road, all the way to the Stuart Highway. When we got to Kulgera, they said the Palmer and Finke rivers were flowing over the bridge. When we got to the Palmer, we had to wait a while for the water to go down so we could get across. We finally got to Alice Springs late. Our new house on the east side of town had nothing in it, so we just dropped our swags and camped there that first night.

I had a month to settle in before starting work at the IAD. What I remember most about that time was how our two daughters managed being back in a town after living at Mimili. Karina was only about five years old, so she'd spent most of her life in the bush, and she missed her little friends. She'd go to kindergarten, playing with the kids, and just talk Yankunytjatjara all the time. One day I was in my room and I could hear Karina and some kids outside playing. They'd found a big perentie, a big *ngintaka* had come down from the hill near our place and was walking on the road. All the kids were saying: "Hey, look at that big lizard!" Then I heard Karina: "Lizard *wiya*, *kuka palatja*! [That's no lizard, it's meat!]" She was so lovely. I always tell her

138

that story and she always says, "Oh, Dad, that's shame job."

She was learning English at school and playing with the kids, and I suppose her friends sort of understood her. Then, one day, her brother Leroy – he was ten or eleven – put his hand on her shoulder and said: "Look, Karina. You gotta talk English. You can't be talking Yankunytjatjara all the time. This isn't Mimili." But all my kids still know Yankunytjatjara, along with their second language, English. Karina even corrects me on my English pronunciation.

When I started work, Jim Downing stayed with me and showed me the ropes for about four weeks. I thought it was going to be a hard job but I knew I would be working with a team, and that's what I liked. I knew a little bit about organising and talking to people from my experience at Mimili. And what I learned there was when you're talking to people doing the work you've got to give and take. You've got to be flexible, not just say, "You do this and that." That's how I wanted to work, anyway. All right, with some people you've got to be firm, and they understand because that's how they're trained. Or I might not be very clear in what I was saying, but I knew what I wanted in my mind. They would say to me: "Look, you gotta tell me straight. You gotta hit me like with a hammer, you know. That's the way I learned." So, as acting director, I was going to try to use those ideas and learn from the staff at the same time.

IAD had eight programs doing two main things: Aboriginal adult education and language training. Teaching Aboriginal languages – Pitjantjatjara, Warlpiri, Pintupi, Arrernte – went two ways: for non-Aboriginal people, and for Aboriginal people who wanted to learn another language or those that had lost their language. It wasn't their fault if they had lost their language, that was just the situation they found themselves in. So, all the teachers at IAD were adult educators, and very good at it. Because of that, I thought: "All right, they've got to be able create things, have imaginative ideas about how to teach Aboriginal people community development, reading and writing, running the community office and store, and things like that. So, I'll give them a little bit of a long rein. If they go too far sometimes, I'll pull the rope in a bit." Turned out that it worked well with them – and for me.

I had some other ideas too, about new programs that I wanted to see started at the IAD. One of the problems for us at Mimili (and I knew it was the same on other Aboriginal-owned cattle properties) is that we didn't have the management skills to run a business like that: no training in accounting or marketing. And Aboriginal people needed more education in doing things like repairing bores and windmills, saddle-making, stock management, and bookkeeping. They should know about new methods of horse breaking and other ideas that were coming out. I didn't have a name for the program, but I knew a fella who worked for the Chief Minister's Department in Darwin who could do it: Stewie Phillpot. I called him up when I was back in Alice Springs, told him my idea and said: "You know, IAD hasn't got a lot of money to pay you. But we can give you a little bit, so you won't go hungry. I know you're working for the Chief Minister's Department, making good money, but I need help." He said he'd think about it, and later he told me he'd take the job. He worked at the IAD for peanuts, and I know it was hard for him and his family living for four years in an expensive place like Alice Springs.

Me and Stewie sat down and put our ideas together, and later on he got funding from the Aboriginal Development Corporation. It was a four-year certificate course and he called it the "Rural Extension Program of the IAD". Six other people worked on that, and they ran courses everywhere. Stewie even went as far as Warburton in Western Australia. There were courses on horse breaking, spaying old cows, testing for pregnancy, and all the other things I mentioned. They had other ideas too, like organising a survey of camels and giving a certificate course on stock inspecting. They did a good job. But it went only four years until ADC cut the funding.

I was also thinking about the Cross-Culture Group. One day I had an idea of how to start up something like that again. This church minister rang me up from Sydney and said that thirty-five American university students and their two professors were arriving in Australia in three weeks. They wanted to do a course on Aboriginal culture. He told me he couldn't find anything like that anywhere, but he heard from the Nungalinya Bible College in Darwin that maybe the IAD offered a cross-culture course for volunteer workers on Aboriginal communities. So I told him we had the course, no worries. But we didn't, not yet anyway.

At that time I believed it was a good thing for people coming from overseas to learn about Aboriginal language, culture, and how they lived. And I thought that, later on, when they become qualified in law or accounting or whatever they're studying, they might come back and work for Aboriginal people. We needed more skilled workers.

So, I called Peter Willis, the head of the Community Development Program, and said, "Righto, brother, we got this cross-culture course for non-Aboriginal people."

"What?"

I thought I'd play around with him a bit. "Oh, you forgot, Peter?" And then I explained what was happening.

"No. No way," he said. "I will not start a cross-culture course for a bunch of Yanks coming from…" It was a very important university, but I still can't remember the name.*

Oh, all right Peter. "OK *Palya*. Just thought I'd ask you." Then I did it myself.

When he left, I sat down with my secretary and made a program: IAD Cross-Culture Course. I had to bullshit on the telephone. Talked to different people, worked out the speakers I was going to have, what days and what time and all that. And I put Peter Willis in the course too. In a couple of days, my secretary typed it all out – she was a very smart secretary – and I called Peter Willis to come and see me.

I showed it to him and said, "Yeah, that's it. You're going to run it." There were about eighteen speakers lined up. I was on four times: welcoming everybody, and talking about early white settlers, Pitjantjatjara and Yankunytjatjara, and Aboriginal work on the cattle. Geoffrey Shaw from Tangentyere was there; Mike Last

* Peter can: it was Puget Sound University

from Pitjantjatjara Council; Bob Randell from Legal Aid. Biggest problem was that we had too many speakers and only five days.

When the students arrived, everything was ready. It was a hectic five days but we survived it, and when it was over they all thought it was really good. The professors and students were thanking us and telling us how much they appreciated it. Peter Willis took all the glory and that was all right. I said to him, "Good on you, Pete." After that, he ran the program four times a year and he loved it.

I think those were two of the best things I did when I was at the IAD. There was another new program that started up while I was there and that was interpreter training. It was Dr Jim Wafer's idea and I thought it was something Aboriginal people needed to learn. After a lot of talking to the national body in Canberra, IAD was able to run accredited courses.

In 1980 Jim Downing decided not to come back, so the board made me full-time director. By 1984 the IAD was becoming more of a town-based organisation. We weren't doing much in South Australia any more. Technical and Further Education (TAFE) was working together with us there, and they were taking it over. We decided to have an internal review of the IAD at that time: looking at how the director should be working with the heads of the programs and the kinds of things we should be teaching. David Hope did the first review, and a lot of good changes came out of that. Then Brian Doolan and Dr Dick White wrote another report and came up with fifty-four recommendations, which we used to make more important changes in the way IAD was running.

I kept working until 1986, when I said to the board that I was running out of ideas and that IAD needed another person to lead them through. The staff was very dedicated – working long hours, no overtime pay – very skilled workers, and a good mob to work with. The board accepted my resignation and they chose Barbara Flick as the new director. Since then Darryl Pearce took over, and now the director is Helen Liddle. I think I made the right decision to leave, because there's a lot of wonderful things happening at the IAD in the way of courses.

Barbara, Darryl and Helen and their staff really got it up and running. Every course that Aboriginal people do, they get a certificate so they are really qualified. And even if there's no certificate for the Cross-Culture Course, I'm happy to say it's still going strong.

They were good years for me at the IAD and I'm really proud to be part of its development. And a lot of the credit goes to the board and the staff, because from almost the first day as acting director more and more of my time was spent in doing work outside. Those were the years of land rights.

uwa – yes
kuka palya – meat's OK

Land Rights

It's not easy for me to talk about land rights, mainly because there are so many things to remember.

It all started during those four years I was at Mimili. In about 1976 Pitjantjatjara people round Amata way started up a new organisation. I heard they were calling it Pitjantjatjara Panorama Council, or something like that. It was their idea – a Pitjantjatjara idea – and that was all right. I'm true-blue Yankunytjatjara man, so I kept away from their business. Some of the old Yankunytjatjara fellas from Mimili used to go to the meetings, and when they got back I'd tell them that it was the Pitjantjatjara Council and had nothing to do with them. But then my thinking changed.

Soon after the Loan Fund Commission bought the Mimili pastoral lease, they surrendered the land to the South Australian Government. Somehow, Don Dunstan, the Premier of South Australia then, got in touch with me by telegram, saying that Mimili was now Crown Land, and I should go over to the South Australian Aboriginal Land Trust. I wasn't sure what to do, but I told the Mimili Council that, in my opinion, the land shouldn't be held by an organisation working out of Adelaide. It was better for the people themselves to hold the papers for the land. So I thought we should get a lawyer to act for us. I had heard that the Pitjantjatjara Council was talking about land rights, and I thought maybe we should contact them. The Mimili Council agreed.

I phoned Paul Everingham's law firm in Alice Springs and talked to Peter, a lawyer I knew there. I explained the situation to him and he agreed to act for the Mimili Cattle Company. I also heard that Don Dunstan was coming up to Mimili and other communities in the north-west of South Australia to talk

144

about a Pitjantjatjara Land Rights Working Party he had just set up. The chairman was going to be Chris Cocks, and working with him would be Ross Howie – a lovely man, and a lawyer for the Central Land Council – and David Hope.

The first time I was involved with the Pitjantjatjara Council was when they decided to hold a meeting at Mimili. A lot of people were there, sitting and talking over three days, and it looked very good to me. I didn't say anything at the meeting: I was just listening and learning. They were talking about the land, about the Land Rights Working Party, about getting back for themselves all the Pitjantjatjara, Yankunytjatjara, and Ngaanyatjarra land in South Australia. It was the first time I met Tony David – he worked for a long time for the Pitjantjatjara Council – and Phillip Toyne, their lawyer. They told me later that I treated them coolly, like I wasn't happy about what was going on. That must be right, but I thought I was good to the both of them.

I could see that there was good political reasons for joining the Pitjantjatjara Council, especially if we were going to talk about land rights for Mimili. After the meeting I went to my Yankunytjatjara relations and said: "I think we should join, go in with the Pitjantjatjara Council and go to their meetings. Then, all together, we can become strong for land rights. If it's just us, the Government won't listen." They could understand what I was saying, especially Pompey Everard and Tommy Tjampu – two of the most senior Yankunytjatjara men at Mimili. But for me there were still some things that I didn't like. I'd see my good friend Bill Edwards – he was the Pitjantjatjara Uniting Church minister for many years – and say to him: "Hey, look. I think it's gammon about this Pitjantjatjara Church and Pitjantjatjara Council. You know we're all different. We're Yankunytjatjara, and that's not the same as Pitjantjatjara. We're not all Pitjantjatjara people. This is gammon, you know." It was the same as the Education Department calling the school at Mimili the Pitjantjatjara School. I'd say: "Look, it's just not right. You are on Yankunytjatjara land. It's not Pitjantjatjara." I think they listened to me, because it was later called the Mimili

Pitjantjatjara and Yankunytjatjara School.

I didn't have much more to do with them until after I left Mimili in 1979. That year the Mimili, Fregon, and (I think) Indulkana communities appointed me their representative on the Pitjantjatjara Council. So they had me then: I couldn't do anything else but work for them. I was happy for that, but I still went on saying that we couldn't use the word "Pitjantjatjara" all the time. We had to find a word that included everybody. They never did find one, and from time to time there would be problems.

Punch Thompson – the Pitjantjatjara Council chairman – really got under my skin at a meeting at Ernabella. There were a lot of white people listening, and for their benefit he said: "OK. There's a Yankunytjatjara boundary, but it's like a mark with a pencil. You can easily rub it out. When the Pitjantjatjara people came in, we took over and put another boundary with ink, with a biro. So now it's stronger, harder to rub out."

When I heard that I just saw red, and I wasn't going to let him get away with it. Right in the meeting I stood up and told him that wasn't right. Hughie Cullinan was sitting beside me, trying to stop me: "Don't, don't. Just leave it." But was I going to just sit there, let Punch have his way, and nobody say anything? I had to speak up, so I told him: "Look. Yankunytjatjara people have a big area. When the Pitjantjatjara people came in, there was a drought, and the Yankunytjatjara people were afraid of a fight, so they just ran away, east towards the railway line. And you Pitjantjatjara people killed us off just about, then took our land, you know?" It was a bit heavy, but it had to be said.

I'd been back from Mimili for two months when the South Australian Minister for Mines, Hugh Hudson, put out a press statement saying they found oil at a place called Mt Byilcaoora. It's near Tjanmatapanpatjaranya, north of Wallatina. The minister was asking companies to let the Government know if they were interested.

The Pitjantjatjara Council didn't know what was going on, so the executive and the Council lawyer, Phillip Toyne, went down to Adelaide. We got out of the plane at six in the evening and we were at Hugh Hudson's office by seven. It was the first time I worked for the Council, and the first meeting I'd been to with a government minister about land rights. We listened to him, then we said: "Look. Your government hasn't done anything about our claim for land rights yet and we can't be dealing with mining companies until we know what's going to happen about our claim." Everybody knew that the Land Rights Working Party report was finished and the Government already had what they called a draft Pitjantjatjara Land Rights Bill. After the meeting the Pitjantjatjara Council made a press statement saying that it was too early for the Government to get excited about oil because we were still negotiating for land rights. Nothing happened after that, and they never did find oil at Tjanmatapanpatjaranya.

The Labor Government of South Australia called an election in that year, and lost. At first the new Liberal Government went quiet on land rights. Then the new Premier of South Australia, David Tonkin, announced that there was going to be a new committee to negotiate or register sacred sites on Pitjantjatjara Council members' land in South Australia, especially on Granite Downs. The committee was then going to look after those places for Anangu. There were going to be three people on it: Les Nayda, an Aboriginal person from the Office of Aboriginal Affairs; Colin Gatehouse, from the Department of Mines and Energy; and Barry Lindner, the community adviser from Yalata.

Phillip Toyne rang me up at the IAD wanting to talk about the Government's announcement. We thought it'd be a good idea if I got on the transceiver radio and tried to organise a meeting at Amata. So Phillip flew me down, and I told the people what the new Government did by announcing a committee to look at sacred sites. They weren't interested in land rights, I said, just spots on a map. Then Phillip reckoned: "Look, I think it's a good time now. We should think about going down, hiring buses and going down to meet the government people in Adelaide." Everybody agreed and they made a decision to go ahead and organise it.

From that day at Amata, I became really involved with the Council. I became one of the interpreters at meetings in the

147

bush and in Adelaide; I was one of the people talking to the Government on land rights, and talking to our professional people, especially Phillip Toyne. And the IAD was really good to me, letting me go to all those meetings. I'd go back after being away maybe a week and I'd explain to the IAD board about what was happening. And because the IAD board supported land rights for Aboriginal people, they said that was quite right I should be involved. I think it was Dr Trevor Cutter who said that the IAD director should be going to land rights meetings in his own right, not just because he's an interpreter. I was doing both anyway, but I really appreciated their support.

It was going to take a lot of money to have a full Pitjantjatjara Council meeting in Adelaide. We talked to Mike Last – he's probably worked the longest for the Council – and he got us financial support from the Uniting Church in Australia. The IAD also chucked in with money they had from the Australian Council of Churches. With their help, we managed to hire three buses and three Toyotas. No money came from the Government.

And we talked to people down south. One woman who was really supportive was Ruby Hammond, then the Director of the Aboriginal Legal Rights Movement. She really stuck her neck out to help the Pitjantjatjara Council on land rights. She got some of her people behind her, and organised the food and second-hand clothes. She talked to the South Australian Jockey Club – they were very good to us – and arranged for us to camp and have our meeting on the lawn of the Victoria Park Racecourse. She just went out of her way for us, and did a terrific job. It turned out later that a lot of Aboriginal people in Adelaide were against what she was doing. I suppose they might have been a bit jealous of what she did for us Anangu. Or maybe they thought she wasn't spending enough time helping her own people in the Adelaide area and the Riverland. She got into a lot of trouble with the Board of the Aboriginal Legal Rights Movement, and in the end she had to resign. But the Pitjantjatjara Council people will always remember what she did for them.

When I got back from that meeting in Amata, I rang up Les Nayda, the Aboriginal person who was going to be on that

148

government sacred sites committee. I told him what had happened: "We aren't very happy with the Government's new committee. It's not going to help Pitjantjatjara land rights. It's only to put a fence around sites and that's not the land rights we're talking about." I said that the chairman, Punch Thompson, and Ivan Baker – one of the first people to start the Council – were not very happy either. They had known Les as far back as 1970, and wanted to know what he was going to do.

These are Les's own words to me: "OK, I'll put my head on the block. I'm prepared to resign from that committee and give my support to the Pitjantjatjara Council." He asked me if I could organise a meeting with Punch Thompson and the others when we were in Adelaide so he could explain himself. I really respected him for doing that: he was a government bloke on a government committee, but he was prepared to stick his neck out. In the end, I don't think that committee had one meeting.

We knew we had to move quickly, and by February everything was ready for Adelaide. Everybody was to meet at Indulkana, so me and Gary Lewis went ahead in the IAD bus, the two larger buses would meet us the next day. In the morning, Phillip Toyne, Mike Last, and somebody else arrived with the three Toyotas. Then our little bus was taken for the women to use, and me and Gary were just left there with our swags, tucker box, and no vehicle. Everybody wanted to go, and they were trying to make room on the buses for them. I finally said to somebody: "Look, that's all right. I'll go back to Alice and I might catch the plane down." Of course, when Phillip found out, he said: "Oh, no! You gotta be here! You gotta be in this party." We managed to get a ride in one of the Toyotas.

It was pretty late when we got going, and it was slow following each other on the old Stuart Highway. That first night we camped just south of Mt Willoughby Station. Early next morning, I was just lying in my swag listening to all the senior people, those *tjilpi*, talking *aalpiri*, you know, singing out to each other from their campfires. They were discussing the land rights issue and what might happen with the Government. Then I could hear a group of people from Ernabella gathered over at one camp, having a Bible reading in Pitjantjatjara. Their prayers were for the Government to listen to them, and for Aboriginal people to stay calm and not be aggressive. They prayed like that in Pitjantjatjara. They thanked God for the nice morning and asked God to bless them on the trip, look after them along the way. When they finished, we started off again.

Phillip Toyne was travelling ahead, and as we got close to Coober Pedy, he sent word to us on his radio that there were journalists waiting outside the town. The vehicle I was in was always last, and when I got there, they were interviewing some *tjilpi* and taking pictures for the television. We stayed in Coober Pedy only long enough to get stores, then kept going, driving slow. It was a hot, dry, thirsty day. We got to Kingoonya late, but went on, and finally stopped a bit north of Port Augusta. It was about one in the morning and we just dropped our swags and slept anywhere. I don't know about the people on the buses, but I didn't like this trip. There were too many people in our Toyota and no room for a good-looking fat man like me to stretch out.

When we got up next morning, everybody was worried. The white people living in Port Augusta must've seen us on their televisions. They were on the radio, talking about wild blackfellas coming down. All bullshit. When we were in town getting fuel and stores, more journalists were interviewing people. We left Port Augusta with no trouble, Phillip Toyne still in the lead.

I think we might've been close to Port Pirie when people in our car saw Phillip coming back. Now what was it? He's pretty upset and asks us if we've seen his dog, his good friend Blue. No, nobody's seen him. "Oh, yeah," I thought, so I called out to him: "Hey, *tjuu*. Don't worry about the dog. Worry about the land. Land rights! *Mantaku!*" He just drove away. Never even answered me.

We finally got to Adelaide. Lined up, driving real slow down the Main North Road, I could hear motor cars going "beep, beep". Buses, trucks, taxis, they did that all the way to the city. They knew we were coming, and it was just fantastic. We made our way to Victoria Park Racecourse. I'd been there before, but this time it was for land rights. When we arrived, all our Adelaide Aboriginal people were there, all the Nangkas. There were hundreds waiting for us. When those Pitjantjatjara, Ngaanyatjarra, and Yankunytjatjara people unloaded themselves from the buses, food was right there for them. My cousin, Eileen Cooper, was waiting with her family – she hadn't seen her uncle, Kanytji, since 1972 – and they had a happy reunion. Television was there, and people from the newspapers, and it was fantastic. I'm not sure, but I think we were all camping on the racecourse. All I know is that it was hard ground. That night, people put on *inma* – you know, singing and dancing. And every night after that there was *inma*.

I remember Les Nayda turned up that first night, and had a meeting with his old mates Punch and Ivan and (I think) Donald Fraser. No whitefellas involved. He told them he was resigning from that committee. He wanted to listen to Anangu and work with them. "I'm still working for government," he said, "but I'll do whatever I can to help." And he did. Punch became his friend again, and I really congratulate Les for the position he took.

Besides the Nangkas, we found out there were a lot of white people in Adelaide supporting Pitjantjatjara land rights. The Uniting Church and Anglican Church were right behind us, and I think the Catholic too. The newspapers and radio and television were really good. Don Dunstan, the former premier of South Australia, came and talked with us, showing his support, not having anything to do with the Government but as an interested individual.

Now, like I said, there were a lot of things going on and I didn't take a diary or anything, so I might be forgetting a lot. But I think it was the day after we arrived that the new Premier of South Australia, David Tonkin, was going to come to see us. So, first of all, we had our own meeting – like a proper Pitjantjatjara Council bush meeting, only this time it was in the city – working out how we were going to start talking to the Government. When he arrived with his advisers there was a big crowd at the racecourse. Dr Tonkin said he was willing to meet with the executive of the Pitjantjatjara Council, and to start a round-table discussion about what could be done. I thought he was very good, and the other Anangu seemed happy. The premier and the Minister for Aboriginal Affairs, Harold Allison, and the other government people were invited to *inma* that night.

Unfortunately, when the meeting ended and the premier started to walk away, a sad thing happened. This man threw a custard pie in the premier's face. The police were there and just jumped on him. Anangu got a fright, and I could hear them saying: "Hey? He's *mayatja pulka*, a big boss, so why did that fella do that?" And those *tjilpi* told me to apologise to the premier for what happened. They wanted him to know that it was not their doing. So I passed it on, and David Tonkin went up to the old fellas and said: "I know that. No, I know it's nothing to do with you people." Still, it was too bad for us, because I knew we were going to miss out on the headlines in the newspapers. The custard pie was going to take it away, become the major story on the front page, and that's what happened.

Later on, the executive met with the premier, his deputy, Roger Goldsworthy (the Minister for Mines and Energy), and Harold Allison, and other government advisers. Dr Tonkin said that we had to put everything on the table, like playing cards. We were asking for twelve or fifteen things. Our idea was for Anangu to talk first, then our lawyer would come behind and negotiations would start. So we did that, and I was asked to thank the premier for seeing us and for his co-operation. Blah, blah, blah. And he said the same thing. Then I asked Phillip Toyne to proceed, and he went through the Pitjantjatjara Council position on land rights. It was very good. The government people listened to it and said: "Right, we'll take that. Now this is the Government's position on all those things." They agreed not to set up that sacred sites committee, and they said that further negotiations on land rights would be directly between the government people and their advisers and the Pitjantjatjara Council, its executive and advisers. After that, we all shook hands and said it was a very fruitful discussion. We promised the Government that we would keep some of what was said confidential to the journalists. When we got back to Victoria Park, we reported to all the people and said we didn't promise anything, and the Government didn't either. Both sides just put ideas forward, and said they'd keep talking.

Soon after, we left to return to our homelands in the bush. But it was only the start of negotiations between us and the Government. It was all new to me, and I found it educational. I was learning and taking more notice. And I was becoming more and more involved. But I chickened out of the trip back to Alice Springs by road and got myself an air ticket. Took me an hour and fifty minutes on the jet. The modern Yankunytjatjara bloke!

It was about two months later when some of us went back to Adelaide. This time a lot of executive members and others went – too many really. We managed to get some funding to cover our expenses, but in order to save some money we stayed at Mulganya, run by Aboriginal Hostels. It was good, cheap accommodation, and Mr and Mrs Rankin, the managers, gave us just what we needed: good food to eat and a good bed to sleep. They looked after us really well.

At that second meeting, the premier was there along with his two ministers – Roger Goldsworthy and Harold Allison. I think Graham Gunn, the Member for Eyre, was there too. I was asked to start the ball rolling again, so the lawyers could come behind. And I remember becoming really emotional talking to those government people. I talked strongly about Granite Downs. Then I started saying really hard things. I told them that first they smoked us out in 1953 by running that Maralinga bomb testing program, now they won't let us have the land back.

Of course, I know now I was wrong. Maralinga had nothing to do with the South Australian Government at that time. The Commonwealth Government of the late prime minister of Australia, Bob Menzies, had made a secret agreement with the British. They kept it secret from us, living around there, and they kept it secret from Australian white people. I suppose on that day with David Tonkin and the others I was thinking about the times when Aboriginal people didn't count for anything.

153

When cattle and sheep were more important, and when dropping bombs were more important than people.

I was really pushing for Granite Downs from the start of the land rights negotiations. When I finished talking, the premier made a speech, then Phillip Toyne talked. We had a break about then, and I went down to the toilet with Mike Last and Les Nayda. Les was in all the negotiations as an officer in the state Department of Aboriginal Affairs. Lovely Mike Last said to me: "Tjilpi. Look, you're all right now. Mr Tonkin heard you, what you said about Granite Downs. He'll go away and talk to members of his party. So you're OK now. You don't have to say anything else. They got the door open, and you got your foot in. I feel confident something will happen for you." It turned out to be very good advice from Mike Last. And Les Nayda, my bros, said the same thing. I was worked up, but I could hear what they were saying.

Still, you know the history. I don't have to tell you what happened when that *kunmanara* arrived over two hundred years ago. You know his name. I don't want to say it. Sometimes I wonder why Aboriginal people always have to justify themselves, prove themselves to white people. Not just with land rights, but on all kinds of things. You know, I think life is more easy for white people. They don't have to try and prove who they are, where they come from, what language they speak. And that's just what I had to do right through those negotiations with the South Australian Government. I found it very hard to come to terms with, but we had to do it.

The talking went on for some time that day, and it kept going on for months and months. I don't know how many times we went to Adelaide. After the second meeting with the Government, we decided that only a few Anangu needed to go and they could report back to the Pitjantjatjara Council. It seemed like a lot of discussion went on between our lawyers and the government lawyers, working out some fine point so that our wishes and the Government's ideas would be part of the agreement. I was trying to interpret all they were saying, and sometimes when we didn't understand the government people, we'd ask for a ten-minute break. They'd go out, and we'd stay in the room, with Phillip and our other advisers trying to explain. And sometimes, the government lawyers would come up with a new idea and we'd say, "All right, we can't say now but we'll take it back." One time it was really important, so we hired a small plane in Adelaide and flew all the way to Ernabella for a meeting.

We had four advisers involved in the land rights struggle with us. At first, there was Phillip Toyne of course, and Mike Last. Then we had Daniel Vachon, an anthropologist, who we asked to come back from Canada. He had done a lot of work in the Indulkana area and on Granite Downs. So he had experience with Yankunytjatjara people and with the country that looked to be the hardest to get back. The last person was another lawyer, Ron Castan. Phillip felt he needed help with the legal side; he'd always say he was just a bush lawyer. I'm sure he was just having a joke – taking the mickey out of me. But it turned out Ron was a good choice: he was a very clever QC from Melbourne and was a great help in getting a good agreement with the Government.

To me there was one other adviser for us, and that was Les Nayda. Every meeting we'd see him, and it must've been sad for him, as an Aboriginal person, looking at an Aboriginal executive on one side of the table and he was with a white government on the other. And when we'd have a break, he'd have to walk out with those government people, leaving behind the Aboriginal group he supported. But he was very helpful to me, and it was good to have the Government's views explained by someone from the inside. Unfortunately, Les Nayda and Phillip Toyne didn't see eye to eye, professionally that is. Anyway, Les used to help me out, so that was good enough. And I told the Pitjantjatjara Council lawyer.

I didn't know a lot about the government side. David Tonkin came to only some of the negotiations, and he seemed fair to me. You might remember that he once performed a corneal graft on one of my eyes. Another one on their team that was easy to approach was the Attorney-General, Trevor Griffin. He might not have always agreed with us, or liked what we said, but he

155

always listened. Harold Allison, the Minister for Aboriginal Affairs, seemed to be a little behind the Minister for Mines and Energy, Roger Goldsworthy.

I remember this one negotiation was going on for some time, something about mining on Granite Downs again. I was in Adelaide with Phillip, and my friend Donald Fraser, who was also on the Pitjantjatjara Council executive committee, was helping me. At the meeting, the Minister for Mines and Energy said to me: "But you're not a real Aborigine. You don't live at Wallatina, you live in Alice Springs." He really hit me between the eyes. I just couldn't understand what he was on about, so I said: "Whaddya think a real Aborigine is? Would I be a real Aborigine if I came down here arguing for my land with you, sitting around this table wearing nothing but a red headband and a lap-lap?" I wanted to have more argument with him, but the meeting was breaking up. Phillip heard what he said, and he was fuming. Donald Fraser was pretty upset, I think because he sort of felt that what the minister said might be for him too.

Granite Downs took a long time to work out, and the main reason — but not the only one it turned out — was that it was owned by one of the largest land-holders in South Australia — the McLachlan family. During one of our meetings, Hugh McLachlan came and made us an offer. He said: "I will agree to give Wallatina to the Pitjantjatjara people if I can have the bottom end of Kenmore Park." As I said, Kenmore Park had been purchased by the Aboriginal Loan Fund Commission in 1975, and we wanted it to be part of the land rights package. After Hugh McLachlan had his say, we all left for lunch at the Aboriginal Legal Rights Movement offices.

There were quite a few of us there: Donald Fraser, Gary Lewis, Ivan Baker, Punch Thompson, Robert Stevens and our advisers. Phillip said: "You people better think about what Mr McLachlan said. Have a good talk about it." We knew we had an important decision to make. Punch Thompson, Ivan Baker and Donald thought it was a good idea. They were happy to agree with McLachlan so that I could have Wallatina. But I said: "No. You hang onto Kenmore. You've got it now, don't give it back to the whitefellas. We can wait. As Yankunytjatjara people, we can wait for Granite Downs. And my brother-in-law, Ivan Baker, said: "Wait a minute, *tjuu*. That's your *ngura*, your place. We're all right. We'll get our land, but you won't have Wallatina." "No," I said, "We'll wait." So we went back to the Government and told them we refused McLachlan's offer.

The South Australian Government then decided to talk to the Commonwealth Government about the Granite Downs issue. There was a Liberal Government in Canberra, same for South Australia, and Hugh McLachlan was a member of the Liberal Party. So he was one of their kind, and they had to talk nice to him. And they made an agreement among themselves (it had nothing to do with us): in return for McLachlan not renewing his pastoral lease in 2008, he would get $338,000 in 1981. On top of that, if he surrendered his lease or when he left in 2008, he'd be paid compensation for all the improvements he had made. The way was finally open then to include Granite Downs in the land rights deal.

When we got back up north, I had to explain McLachlan's offer to Yankunytjatjara people living at Iwantja and Mimili. I told them why I didn't agree with it, and that we wouldn't be getting Granite Downs and Wallatina until maybe 2008. When they heard that, I got into a lot of trouble for not taking McLachlan's offer. They thought it was a fair swap. So my relations weren't very happy. The men were really angry with me and it stayed that way for some time. White people – all my friends working in Aboriginal organisations – don't understand how Anangu can get wild with me. There was nothing I could do but live with it – and hope I'd still be around in 2008.

Naturally the whole business made me unhappy too, and I started thinking that maybe I did make a mistake. 2008 was a long way away. I could've agreed, and my executive friends told me to do just that. Even Donald Fraser was happy to see part of Kenmore Park go over to McLachlan so Yankunytjatjara people could have Wallatina. But what was in the back of my head was this: I think McLachlan was only talking about the 102-square-kilometre paddock around Wallatina Homestead. He was going to give that to me, nobody else, in return for a big part of Kenmore. I tried to tell my relations that, but I don't think they believed me. Anyway, I thought, I was still working for the IAD and I could stay there until things changed.

As it turned out, in 1990 McLachlan advised the Government he wanted to leave early. So we took over Granite Downs. It was a broken-down station and there were a lot of things to fix up: water tanks, windmills, troughs, fences, yards. It was going to take a lot of work and money to start up an Aboriginal-run cattle enterprise. For me, I'm happy to be living at Wallatina again.

But, of course, we didn't know any of that back then. It seemed like there wasn't much left in the way of signing a land rights agreement with the Government. Except for Mintabie. It was the Mintabie Opal Field that took the longest to work out. In the 1950s old Tommy Cullinan had a little bit of a mine at Mintabie – only a pick-and-shovel job. Different people had a go at it before him, but they all left it much like it's always been. Then in the 1960s Coober Pedy miners started going there, and in the 1970s I think it really started up. Pitjantjatjara land rights came a bit late, the miners were already there.

Mintabie is in the middle of Granite Downs Station. In the late 1970s the South Australian Government declared a 100-square-kilometre Precious Stones Field around Mintabie, like Coober Pedy and Andamooka. At the same time the traditional owners of that country and the Pitjantjatjara Council were saying that it is Aboriginal land and they were worried about it.

They were worried for a lot of reasons. At Mintabie, most of the mining is open-cut. There weren't any rules about rehabilitating the environment, planting trees – nothing. They dug their holes, took their money, and got out. But some of them were not getting out, and they are still hanging around. The town is in the middle of a rabbit warren. On our land. That *tjalku wapar* is there and, you know, it's a real thing. Like I said, it holds people's beliefs, their family line and the song line, and that's why they were worried.

Of course, the miners wanted to keep on digging and they

weren't going to let our land rights claims stop them. They were jumping up and down, getting real worked up, and wanting the Government to listen to them too. So, they'd have their separate meetings with the Minister for Mines and Energy and Graham Gunn, their member in parliament. And then we'd have our meetings with the government people. I don't think we ever negotiated face-to-face with the miners, and it was hard to work things out. I remember our executive were getting tired of all the meetings, and sometimes they wouldn't go. And it'd be just me going down with the lawyers and anthropologist. I could understand why they didn't want to go: most of it was technical lawyers' argument, and it didn't seem to really matter. They had business of their own at home. Still, our advisers wanted us to be there, and I'm sorry to say that sometimes it was only me.

It went on and on, until finally it looked like they reached an agreement. The Precious Stones Field would stay there, but it would also be part of the land package to the Aboriginal corporation that was going to be set up – Anangu Pitjantjatjara. Where the town was, the miners would have a living area lease from the Crown. We wanted it to last just fifteen years, but in the end both the Labor and Liberal parties gave them a twenty-one-year lease. I think only Robin Milhouse of the Australian Democrats Party argued for us in parliament.

So in the end we didn't win everything we wanted, but the agreement was better than nothing. And we found out quick enough that the agreement didn't solve all the problems. The miners are still at Mintabie, digging their way to China, I suppose. The Government doesn't do much to control what they do. The Department of Mines and Energy is there, but they don't seem to have much control over the miners. The Department of Lands is supposed to explain the land rights law to them – but they don't. We don't get anything from Mintabie, and government doesn't either. The miners say the Field isn't big enough – they want to go outside – and won't understand why we are unhappy about that.

Anyway, the agreement we had with the Government became the Pitjantjatjara Land Rights Act. On 4 November

1981, at Itjinpiri Creek near Ernabella, we had what the Government called Proclamation Day. Everybody was there – Premier David Tonkin and others from the Government, journalists from Australia and overseas, and Anangu from all over. I'll always remember the premier's speech that day. He said: "All the world and the people of South Australia are watching you and what you're going to do with this land." So I often remind Anangu about that: "They're watching you." If we don't do the right thing on this land, the Government is always watching to take it away. And that's the thing I can't understand. It's hard! We know this has always been our land. We got the stories; we got the culture; we got the language; we got the Law – our own Law. So why is the white man saying we're watching you, watching what we're going to do? The land was ours all the time. OK, we didn't have a piece of paper, but it was still ours. The Federal Government can talk today about "instrument of reconciliation", but I think it's bullshit.

The Government of South Australia did listen to us, but we had to make them listen. And what they did was only for part of the state. All right, it's mainly desert, but it's good desert, and our homeland. Later on, Anangu living at Yalata got their land back too, but, again, their country around Maralinga is desert. The Government never wanted it for anything but testing atomic bombs and other weapons. I'm sorry for other Aboriginal people living in South Australia, those living in the River Country and close to Adelaide. They didn't get land rights. They've only got the Aboriginal Land Trust to speak for them and hold the title to their old reserves.

Still, for the Pitjantjatjara Council, I can congratulate David Tonkin and his government for what they did. Maybe the Queen should make him Sir for that thing.

We all worked hard – our executive members and our professional people. And I'd like to say something about our advisers that helped us get land rights. First, Mike Last – he was only at two meetings with the Government, but he did a lot of work in the background, looking after the money side. And our anthropologist, Daniel Vachon, got the information we needed

160

during the negotiations. One thing I found out: when you're talking to government and you've got a black face and no piece of paper, they can't hear you. If you got the same thing to say, but you're a white professional with a piece of paper, they listen. And I'd like to congratulate our two lawyers, Ron Castan and Phillip Toyne. They'll always be remembered by Anangu for the work they did. Especially Phillip. I always call him champion of the Pitjantjatjara people, or might be Yankunytjatjara and Ngaanyatjarra – you might say champion of this area. I worked a lot with him, and I know he always had concern for Anangu. He was a good mate and a hard worker.

So, we received freehold title under a new law for one hundred and two thousand square kilometres of our land in South Australia. It wasn't all the land the Pitjantjatjara Council wanted to get back. We knew there was still a lot of work to do in Western Australia and at Ayers Rock in the Northern Territory – and I'll get back to that. But on that day at Itjinpiri Creek everybody was happy: at last we've got the whitefellas' piece of paper in our hands. Now we could sit back and enjoy living on the land and going about our own business. There was going to be a new body, Anangu Pitjantjatjara or AP, and with it the traditional owners would manage the land. I still didn't like the name "Pitjantjatjara" on everything, and I don't think the Ngaanyatjarra people in the west do either, but, for now, we have to live with it.

Turned out, that was only one of our problems. Before the dust settled on Proclamation Day, we were into it again.

aalpiri – style of public speaking especially practised in the early morning as people are waking up around campfires

mantaku – for the land

tjalku wapar – rabbit-eared bandicoot dreaming

Present, Past, Future

I suppose our biggest problem really is that there'd always be others that wanted to use our land. And ever since we got it back that mostly meant miners and mining companies. At the same time as Dr Tonkin was giving his speech about everybody watching us, there was a mining company – BHP Haematite – waiting in the wings, wanting to explore for oil in the Officer Basin, south of Mimili and Fregon. It didn't look like anybody but us wanted to do other things with the freehold land, like run cattle. Tourism was pretty small then. It's no surprise that the Anangu Pitjantjatjara Land Rights Act talks about mining more than anything else, and not just at Mintabie, but any kind of mining on Pitjantjatjara Lands.

There's a lot to say about digging up the country – that's how I look at it, and so do a lot of other Aboriginal people. Personally, I'm not against all mining, but I'm against some. Like open-cut. Opal mining is mostly open-cut mining, and a lot of times it's the same with minerals, like gold and platinum, copper, and uranium. But I'm quite interested in companies looking for oil and gas. We found out that they are easy to get on with and they don't make a very big mess. Of course, with any company you need to sit down with them and negotiate a good agreement.

I often talk to Anangu about mining and I know that some people – I'm not sure how many – are quite happy to do mining themselves and even to see others mining on the lands, even open-cut. Some have pegged a claim at Mintabie and they're looking for opals. I don't know if they're getting anything. And way out west others are thinking about digging for chrysoprase, cutting the stones and polishing them, learning about marketing. They say it's for survival: it's for jobs for Aboriginal people.

They say that we've got to do it to get money and what that can give us. Or else we'll always be relying on government funding, and nobody knows how long that will last. So, some people say it's all right for mining companies to come in. It's a danger for them, but they want dollars and Toyotas and independence.

That's what some middle-aged people say, the ones that know about whitefella things. They want a better house, a better motor car, and things like that for themselves and their families. And they have a lot to say, of course. Not so long ago, about ten small companies or individuals were interested in the chrysoprase out near the Western Australian border. I heard that at one meeting, a lot of people, middle-aged people, were talking about opening up new areas, getting more chrysoprase. And those *tjilpi* were just sitting very quiet in the background, just learning I suppose. Then one of the old fellas leaned over to John Tregenza, the community adviser, and said, "If they want to mine, *palya*, all right, but just at the old mine, no new areas." Then he got up and walked away. That's it, that's all he said.

It's not just those *tjilpi*, but there's people from every age-group that don't want anybody at all cutting up the land. The women are especially strong about that. They just want to live on their country and look after it. They want to take the kids and show them the country – just like when I was young. If they start ripping up the countryside for nickel or copper or different things, that claypan will be gone or that rockhole – it used to be there somewhere. And those Anangu, they just keep saying at the different meetings: "Look, that's my father's country, my mother's country. That place there, that's where I was born. And when I die, I'll go back to the land, be buried in the land." They just feel that the land is part of themselves. But there's pressure on them to say yes, and not just from Aboriginal people, from their relations. It's a funny situation, because a lot of pressure comes from outsiders too.

The Government and people in the mining industry are always saying that Aboriginal people are stopping progress. I don't know what, stopping the progress of something. They say that Aboriginal people are sitting on the minerals and they're blocking the mining companies. They never let up the pressure. I suppose to white people in the mining industry and in the Government too, it's all open country. There's not much in it, just looks like desert to them. So it's all right to rip it up and find what they looking for.

And from the raw material they get, what do they do with it? Like uranium: I hear white people say they can use it for energy and for medical things. But we know it's dangerous. Look what happened to the land at Maralinga after the tests. Aboriginal people living in the area, nobody ever talked to them before it happened. I suppose they thought it was just desert. That nobody was living there.

So that was sort of the situation when BHP Haematite started negotiating with us. The Government wanted to get the ball rolling, and we wanted to wait. We weren't happy about talking to a mining company right after we got the land. Under the Act, there are certain things AP should be doing on behalf of its members, and we wanted about twelve months to work things out, to sit down and make a plan of managing the land now that we had freehold title. All right, we knew we had been pretty lucky so far. There wasn't much mining, except for Mintabie and a little bit out west with the chrysoprase. Earlier on there'd been some nickel exploration near the Western Australian border and in the 1960s some companies were looking for oil, but they found nothing they wanted. Still, we were asking for time to work things out first. The Government never gave us a chance.

We started talking. BHP is the largest company in Australia, and we were the new landowners from the white man's paper. We talked about the environment and the vegetation, we talked about the homelands, and we talked about how we were going to look after all those things. We had experts to come in and advise us on the proper ways to go about talking to mining companies. We discussed how best to protect the country and the *wapar*. We had some experience with companies, and we knew they didn't really want to know about what they called "sacred sites". All they wanted was approval for their roads, seismic lines, camps, airstrips, and so on. And that was all right with us, because we didn't want to tell them where our places were. So we'd worked out a method called work-area clearance, and BHP Haematite had no problem with that. We talked about their exploration program: roads they wanted to put in, drilling sites for water, campsites, how many workers – the lot. We talked about what would happen if they found oil, how they'd be putting down a pipeline, maybe to Marla, the nearest rail-head.

After quite a few meetings, everything was agreed except one thing: Anangu wanted up-front money. They wanted compensation for all the things the company wanted to put through on the land: the seismic lines, roads, airstrips, and all that. We were asking for around $1,000,000. Anangu felt that the company would be disturbing their homelands out from Indulkana, Mimili, and Fregon, and that was fair compensation. BHP Haematite didn't agree.

We had been making joint press releases up until then, just to satisfy the journalists. But the negotiations were supposed to be confidential. Instead of that the BHP Haematite boss went to the television and newspapers and really put down the AP members and AP as an organisation. It was made to look bad for us: that we were being pig-headed and didn't want to listen. Then some politicians joined in and rubbished us publicly. After twelve months of talking, negotiations broke down.

There was another election in South Australia about that time, and a Labor Government was voted back. It was good for us, because the new Government told the companies not to worry AP for a while. The negotiations with BHP Haematite really knocked the stuffing out of people, and we needed a chance to think about what we were going to do. As an organisation, AP was already looking pretty bad already.

Things didn't get better right away. At the same time as we were talking with BHP Haematite, AP got into a difficult legal argument with an Aboriginal man by the name of Reverend Bob Brown. He was a member of the Aboriginal Evangelical Fellowship (AEF) and this new Aboriginal group called Mama

Kurunpa. Its chairman was Pastor Ben Mason, a Ngaanyatjarra man from out west, and that's about all we knew about it at first. Both of them were coming on the AP lands to conduct their AEF rallies – preaching and having sing-a-longs. Nobody thought that was a problem and it didn't look like there was anything wrong with what they were doing under the Land Rights Act.

One weekend Pastor Brown and Ben Mason went to Mimili and had an AEF rally out on the football oval. I wasn't there, but this is what I remember about what I was told. After the Christian business, they started talking about Mama Kurunpa. They said it was an Aboriginal mining company, and AP should give them the first go. And if they found anything, they said, ten per cent would go to Mama Kurunpa for God's work, so much percentage would go to the AEF, and the rest would go to AP. I suppose that to a lot of Anangu it must've sounded good. I don't know what sort of mining they were talking about, but whatever it was, we found out later that they didn't have any financial backing. They reckoned they had help from some very rich people in the Festival of Light.

Then they moved on to Fregon. The AP chairman at that time, Donald Fraser, heard about what they said at Mimili, so he drove down to Fregon to see what was happening about this mining company. When he got there, they were having their AEF meeting in the creek. That was all right, and Donald waited for them to finish. Then he had a word with Pastor Bob Brown and asked him if he had a permit to be on the AP lands. He didn't have one.

So Donald had him prosecuted under the Act. There was a court case about it in Oodnadatta. Bob Brown's lawyers argued that the Pitjantjatjara Land Rights Act went against the Racial Discrimination Act. Our lawyers argued that there's a permit system for entry on the Aboriginal freehold land. People who are not Pitjantjatjara, Yankunytjatjara, or Ngaanyatjarra got to have a permit. Same for Aboriginal people and white people. Bob Brown was an Aboriginal man, but he was not a member of those three groups, so he needed a permit.

I remember during the negotiations with the South Australian Government having an argument with Phillip Toyne on this one. I didn't think it was right that other Aboriginal people had to have a permit. I said permits should only be for white people. But Pitjantjatjara people told me I was thinking the wrong way. They pointed out, and rightly so when I thought about it later, that an Aboriginal person from a different place could come on the lands and be working for a mining company. If he needs a permit, we have control. If there was Anangu business and Aboriginal people from other places were involved, then they could come through without a permit. I lost that argument, and it wasn't the first time. After all, I was only one Yankunytjatjara and there were a lot of Pitjantjatjara.

Coming back to the court case. The magistrate in Oodnadatta made a judgment in AP's favour. Pastor Bob Brown appealed, and it moved down to the Supreme Court in Adelaide. His lawyers made the same argument – that he was being discriminated against – and they won. AP had to appeal to the High Court. The judges there decided seven to nil on the side of AP. Still, I think it clouded up the whole Pitjantjatjara Land Rights Act. The problem is still there, I think, hanging somehow.

While all this was happening – and remember, we're still negotiating with BHP Haematite – Mama Kurunpa wasn't going away. I heard from Les Nayda that they were planning to have a meeting about mining outside the lands so they wouldn't be victimised by AP. I think it was going to be at Marla Roadhouse. I had an idea – nothing to do with anybody else. I was still IAD Director, and from my office I rang up radio telephones on the communities, talked to people on the transceiver radio, trying to get all the Yankunytjatjara people to a meeting at Mimili. I gave them two or three days to organise it, then drove down from Alice Springs with my secretary.

When we got to Mimili, all my Yankunytjatjara relations were there, and some Pitjantjatjara too. I knew what I wanted to say, so I got up on top of the Toyota. Everybody was down on the ground, looking up at me. It was like I had some special authority, sitting up there like – I don't know – like a king. So

I talked and talked, all in Yankunytjatjara, and again in English for the minutes: "We gotta problem," I said to them. "We got this AP Act to look after all the members on this freehold land. We got a problem with this mob, Mama Kurunpa. You know that our chairman charged one of their members with having no permit." I could tell they were all listening to me, so I went on: "Today, we gotta form a Yankunytjatjara Council. We'll have executive members and so on to block Mama Kurunpa coming in the front gate. And the front gate I'm talking about is Marla." The other gate, on the freehold, was Indulkana or Iwantja. Both places are on Yankunytjatjara land. I think I must've sounded like Winston Churchill.

I had strong support from the meeting, especially from people like Albert Lennon. Everybody was speaking up, saying things like "Yep. That's it. We gotta stop Mama Kurunpa coming on the AP lands. We gotta stop that mining company. We got enough problems with this whitefella mining company, let alone having problems with our own people." And some said, "We haven't had a chance to work it out yet, what we gonna do on our freehold land." There was a lot of good stuff like that they were saying. After lunch we picked the executive members. Albert Lennon turned to me and said, "What about you?" But I said no, I think because I didn't want to be seen up front. I'd be a member and support the Council, but with no executive hat on. So they picked the executive. I can't even remember who they were. But I do remember when it was: Ash Wednesday, the day of the terrible bushfires.

We were feeling really happy for ourselves. When I went back to Alice Springs, I got the Pitjantjatjara Council lawyer to draw up the constitution, and some money was paid to become a legal body. The Yankunytjatjara Council had only one aim: to block Mama Kurunpa. And we did, our members did that. The chairman of Mama Kurunpa, Pastor Ben Mason, rang me up and he said: "Right, I agree with you people. It's not going to happen. I put a lid on it, finish." It was good that Pastor Ben Mason was chairman. He's a Ngaanyatjarra, like I said. His people are from out west, and he's part of AP. And I congratulate him for the decision he took and what he did with his own board members on Mama Kurunpa.

After that, people thought the Yankunytjatjara Council could be used to help set up more homelands out of Mimili, Fregon, and Indulkana. The funding agency said it was a good idea, so they got money for a backhoe, water trailer, cherry-picker, Nissan car – all for the Yankunytjatjara homelands. But they worked like that only for a little while. I think people thought there were just too many organisations, so they transferred all those things to AP, or it might have been Pitjantjatjara Council. So the Yankunytjatjara Council, it's on the shelf now. Asleep.

Through all of this, AP managed to come up with a way for there to be mining on the freehold land and solve the problems we had with BHP Haematite. It was actually the idea of the Federal Minister for Aboriginal Affairs, Clyde Holding, and it worked out a lot better than what he did with uniform land rights. He stuffed that up, really. He had a meeting with Phillip Toyne and said AP should think about getting its own exploration licence and farming out to mining companies. Or maybe AP could work with other mining companies in what they called a consortium.

Our advisers thought it sounded good, and it was my job to sell it to the senior people, you know, all the *tjilpi*. It was hard for me to do because I was only a young fella, inexperienced in certain things, didn't really know enough. I couldn't talk to those *tjilpi* straight out like I was the One Who Knew. And I couldn't even make it look like I decided on anything, or else I'd be in big trouble. It was up to them, the Knowledgeable People. Anyway, I got away with it because I said I was only interpreting what Phillip Toyne said.

The meeting was at a place called Yurangka, between Fregon and Amata, on a cold August day in 1984. There were little fires going everywhere. When we got everyone together, Phillip started and I translated: "You know, there are a lot of powerful men out there in the whitefella world, and they're really making a lot of trouble for Anangu Pitjantjatjara." I translated and kept on apologising for talking to all the *tjilpi* that way. We told them about the mining industry making a lot of trouble for Aboriginal people right across the board. The miners were saying that people like them were bad, that Aboriginal people were making things hard for everybody. And they were saying this everywhere they could: on television and radio, in the newspapers, advertising, pamphlets. Anangu didn't know, we said, but we lived in Alice Springs and heard it all the time. I'd listen to the radio and television, and I'd get friends to read the newspaper to me. We told them all that. Then we explained the idea to them, Clyde Holding's idea. We said it might take off some of the pressure. Maybe people should think about looking for oil and gas, because that was easiest to deal with. We talked for a long time, then they asked questions. After lunch we came back, talked again, and more questions. Then that was it: "There it is in a nutshell, men and women. It's up to you."

And we sold it. We left them overnight to think about it, then I heard them talking *aalpiri*. I know I said, early on, that I didn't know much, but this time I was a modern Yankunytjatjara man, and I had a Braille watch. So when they started talking from their campfires, I had a look – just stuck my finger on the watch. Big hand's on the twelve, little hand's on the five. So it was five o'clock. Now, what were they saying? They said at a meeting later on that morning they should do it to make things right with the South Australia Government and the miners. And they told us – the AP executive – to go away and start talking to the companies.

I was still involved after that as an executive member, but the real top dog was Donald Fraser, the AP chairman. First, he got the lawyers, Phillip Toyne and Richard Bradshaw, to start up AP Oil Pty Ltd. Just a two-dollar company. Then they looked around for a partner and, good on them, they found one. It was a big American company called Amoco. Because we never had experience in anything like this before, we got a mining consultant in Adelaide to give us advice. And they wanted to come in as partners too. In the end, AP Oil and three companies made up the consortium. Amoco was the main one because they had all the money.

So we worked through what they called the access agreement to come on AP land, and the partnership agreement. The clearances for the drill site and access road were done by traditional owners and our two anthropologists, Daniel Vachon and Susan Woenne-Green. We got a consultant, Social and Environmental Assessment (SEA), to advise us on rehabilitation and the best ways to go about exploration without damaging too much. Lovely Nadia McLaren and others from SEA did a lot of good work for us on that. And the boss of Amoco in Australia, the late Buddy Waring, turned out to be a good businessman and a good friend of Anangu Pitjantjatjara. He really went out of his way to make the agreement work.

The partners agreed that Amoco would be what they called the operator, and it would have fifty per cent interest. The other two companies would have fifteen per cent each. Now AP didn't have any money, but we had the land. So AP got a twenty per cent carried interest. We didn't have to pay our share until maybe five years down the road, after they found oil or gas. So that was the agreement and it was a good one. AP even won some words of praise from the South Australia Government for what we did.

Sad thing about it was they never found oil or gas. They never really started looking. The access track was built from near Wallatina to Manyura, the drill site, about one hundred and sixty-five kilometres to the west at the end of the Officer Creek. They were going to drill, then something happened. I think the price of oil went too low. Anyway, by 1985 it was all over.

That wasn't the end of it, of course. There are nineteen other mining companies wanting to mine on the lands. The South Australia Government has said that AP has to talk to only one them and the rest have to wait. So that's what's happening now. AP is negotiating an agreement with Plagolmin, a company that wants to look for platinum and other minerals west of Amata, near Kanpi. They say if they find anything, it will be underground mining, not open-cut. But, personally, I don't like it. If the companies get their own way, they'll rip the guts out of the

171

country. We got the Pitjantjatjara Land Rights Act now, but I just don't know how long it's going to last.

* * *

I said before that the Pitjantjatjara Council's main aim was to get the land back for its members. We did that for South Australia first, because we thought it would be the easiest. But still on the agenda was the Ngaanyatjarra side in Western Australia, and Uluṟu – Ayers Rock.

There was one other area and that was Maralinga, what whitefellas called the Woomera Prohibited Area, just south of the AP lands. Before they got the land back, the people of that country lived at Yalata, a mission a long way south of the Trans-Australia railway line and near the sea. They're Pitjantjatjara and Yankunytjatjara people, and my relations from my mother's side. Yalata wasn't their country: they were taken there in the 1950s when the Australian and British Governments used Maralinga to test atomic weapons.

Yalata people weren't part of the Pitjantjatjara Council for a long time, so we weren't involved all that much in land rights for Maralinga. We helped them a bit, and two of our professional people, Phillip Toyne and Daniel Vachon, would go down there and give them advice. I remember I went to one meeting they had, but I was there just to listen. So I don't know much of the details, but they eventually got the land back and started up their organisation called Maralinga Tjarutja. There's a land rights act for their land, but it isn't as strong as the Pitjantjatjara Land Rights Act. I think that's because the South Australian Labor Government knew a bit more when they negotiated the agreement. Maralinga Tjarutja has all the same problems as AP with mining companies and with other things like homelands, health and education. But they've got one other big problem too: how to clean up the mess that the British and Australian Governments left behind when they finished the atomic tests. And I'll get back to that later.

Just after we worked out the land rights agreement with the

172

South Australian Government, Anangu in Western Australia started up their own organisation called the Ngaanyatjarra Council. I wasn't involved in that one either, but in 1982 the Pitjantjatjara Council helped the Ngaanyatjarra people organise a trip to Perth, like we did to Adelaide. Only they didn't do as well. The Liberal Party was in government in Western Australia, and the Liberal Party was always against land rights. The Premier was Mr O'Connor, and the leader of the Labor Party in opposition was Brian Burke.

The Ngaanyatjarra Council had its bush meeting in the city, at the Claremont Show Grounds. I didn't go, but they told me it was a good meeting. Brian Burke went there and he promised he would give them the same land rights as we had in South Australia if the Labor Party was the government. Labor won the next election but, as everybody knows, he didn't keep his promise. The Pitjantjatjara Council and Ngaanyatjarra Council kept working to get the land and, in 1989, the Ngaanyatjarra people finally got something. The Labor Government gave them a ninety-nine-year lease to the Central Reserve and fifty-year lease to some of the land outside. The Ngaanyatjarra Council executive and advisers – our lawyer, Richard Bradshaw, was one of them – worked hard to get a good lease agreement. But we were in a weak position. There are a lot of mining companies that want to come onto that land. The Ngaanyatjarra people have some say about that, but there's no land rights law to protect them, and the pressure is always there.

The area that I still have a lot to do with is the Uluru and Kata Tjuta area, often known as Ayers Rock and the Olgas, which are in the Northern Territory. It's a very important area to Pitjantjatjara and Yankunytjatjara people, especially for Anangu living at Docker River and some in South Australia, and for the people at Mutitjulu, the community right at the Rock. The Government wasn't interested in that land for mining companies, but for tourism, and Uluru and Kata Tjuta have been inside a National Park since 1950.

I think my first involvement with Ayers Rock was with one of my fathers, Paddy Uluru, back in 1971. He was a lovely old fella, married to my auntie Munyi. They were living at Mimili. I went down there with Reverend Jim Downing because Tjilpi Uluṟu sent a message saying he wanted to go back and visit his country, Uluṟu. So we picked him up and took him. When we got there, I met other Aṉangu living in their *kaṉku* close to Uluṟu. The only ones I remembered were Tjilpi Captain and Tiku's mother and father, but I got to know other people from there after our visit. I'd never been to Uluṟu and Kata Tjuṯa before, and Tjilpi Uluṟu told me some of the *wapar* and how important the places were. He told me a story when, a long time ago, he ran away from a policeman who shot and killed his brother right at the Rock. I don't think he ever went back until we were with him.

Some time after that, the Northern Territory Government was thinking about putting a tourist village near Ayers Rock, what we know today as Yulara. I don't know who it was, but somebody dobbed me in to sit on this committee. I forget the name of it. I remember Damian Miller was on it. The committee wanted some Aboriginal people to see where they wanted to put the village, so I organised to have Tjilpi Uluṟu, Captain, and some others taken there. We went and saw the site, and where they wanted to put the airstrip and township. All the old fellas said, no worries, and gave them a clearance for what they wanted to do.

I think it was in 1974 that someone dobbed me in again to interpret for people when they had a look where the new road to Ayers Rock was going to be. They call it the Lasseter Highway today. I went down with a Luritja fella working for the Department of Aboriginal Affairs. At Erldunda we met the engineers, and another DAA bloke with some of the traditional owners for the country along the new highway. So we started off from Erldunda in four or five Toyotas on the old dirt road. They'd show the old people where they wanted to get gravel or do some work, and they would say, "Yes, all right, along here is all right" or "No, you'll have to find somewhere else for the gravel." From Curtin Springs we just went bush – scrub-bashing over the biggest mob of sandhills to where that village is today.

And those *tjilpi* said: "*Wiya*, nothing here. It's just country. All clear."

Then, the Northern Territory Government started up a special working committee to plan what sort of buildings there were going to be at Yulara and I was on it to look after Aboriginal interests. We used to have meetings at one of the old motels at the Rock. This was before any land councils, and I was just a young fella, by myself, and I didn't really know much. I was worried. They weren't really listening to anything I said and I felt like a token blackfella, just there so they could say they talked to Aborigines. I didn't want to be in that situation, so I resigned.

After the Northern Territory Land Rights Act came in, the Central Land Council put in a claim for Ayers Rock National Park and the country around. I was at Mimili then, and Phillip Toyne flew down and asked me if I wanted to be the interpreter on the claim. I agreed, but something must've happened because I didn't do it. They got part of the claim in 1979, but they couldn't get the Park because the Director of Australian National Parks and Wildlife Service (ANPWS) held the papers for it. Ever since then the Pitjantjatjara Council has been working to get the rest of the land back.

Talks with Canberra for land rights at Uluru really began in 1984, and I was a bit involved in that. There were a lot of problems working through the Commonwealth Government, I think because they were so worried about the tourists. The Prime Minister at that time, Bob Hawke, had a change of heart and said he'd give Anangu freehold title under the Northern Territory Land Rights Act. They were hard negotiations. The Government said they wanted a lease so Australian and overseas visitors could still go there. The Park would have to stay under that lease, and it would be managed jointly by Aboriginal people and ANPWS. Anangu agreed and said they'd give a lease for five years, but the Government wanted one for ninety-nine years. It went back and forth like that. In the end the Government made a decision anyway: Anangu had to compromise and give them the ninety-nine-year lease in order to have

Uluru and Kata Tjuta. We got into a little bit of trouble on that, because other Aboriginal people reckoned that it was too long. Anyway, the agreement was signed in 1985.

Anangu wanted to have a big party to celebrate the handing back of Uluru to the Aboriginal people. Pitjantjatjara Council and Mutitjulu community approached me – I was still Director at the IAD – and asked if I would co-ordinate it. But first they wanted me to help explain to everybody what the agreement was and how Uluru and Kata Tjuta were going to be managed. And again the IAD board let me go.

I was to work with Phillip Toyne and a fella from Department of Aboriginal Affairs, and interpret for Tony Tjamiwa – a very strong speaker and one of the traditional owners for Uluru. We were going to all the major cities – Canberra, Adelaide, Melbourne, Sydney – and Tony Tjamiwa would make a speech to the journalists on the radio and television. And we got very good publicity. One of the reasons we had to do it was because the Chief Minister of the Northern Territory, Ian Tuxworth, was going all over the country saying that Ayers Rock should go to his government, not the blackfellas. He was making nasty comments to the press, rubbishing Aboriginal people. Not much different from before: the Northern Territory Government and the Conservation Commission were always behaving like a mob of cowboys. We tried to follow Mr Tuxworth, to be where he was so we could answer what he was saying, but we just didn't have as much money as he did. So in some places we had to use other people to talk for us.

When we got back to Alice Springs, I took eight weeks without pay from the IAD and started co-ordinating the celebration. The Pitjantjatjara Council let me use one of their offices and gave me a secretary. So I thought: "Right, who's gotta be there? Who do we invite to this party?" I decided to ask the biggest mob to come: all the friends of the Pitjantjatjara Council and friends that helped the Pitjantjatjara people at different times. Everybody: both black and white, and government people too. And I got the IAD to invite the Aboriginal education and training organisations right around Australia. I got Congress and

Legal Aid to do the same for the health and Aboriginal Legal Aid side. I invited all the lawyers that helped in the negotiations: Ron Castan, Bruce Donald, and the other lawyers from the Central Land Council, Phillip Toyne and Richard Bradshaw. There were a lot of lawyers involved; and they did a good job.

I talked to the organisations in Alice Springs. Congress would have their medical van there. Tangentyere would set up portable toilets, get water and firewood and set up a camp site. Freda Glynn and Jim Buckle at CAAMA would organise all the media. Bill Davis at Pitjantjatjara Council would set up the sound system for the *inma*. Mutitjulu Community built a big stage, like a big boomerang-shaped embankment. Department of Aboriginal Affairs got an Aboriginal catering service to look after the food side. And Shorty O'Neill and Alfie Presley were going to organise my bodyguards for crowd management. They got all Queenslanders – big fellas – and they were lovely men.

A week before the handback, me and my son, Leroy, drove down to Uluru with a tent and I did the last work from there. Mutitjulu people were busy finishing a video on the Aboriginal story of Uluru. And they had made posters and cards showing Uluru as Aboriginal land. I was getting nervous and excited. I could feel it in the air.

Then the day finally came: 26 October 1985. There were people everywhere. I was up on the stage with some other Anangu, traditional owners for Uluru and Kata Tjuta. There were three flags behind us: the Australian flag, the one for the Northern Territory, and the Aboriginal flag. I could feel a lump in my throat. I tried to talk, but my lips went dry. I knew I had to say something just to control myself and stop the shaking. So I made some announcements and I'd tell everybody: "The Governor-General will be here soon." Things like that. I reckon there must've been four thousand people there. Sir Ninian Stephen, who was Governor-General at that time, arrived and he made a speech. Then they handed over the papers for the Mutitjulu people to sign. Professor Ovington, Director of ANPWS, and someone on behalf of the Commonwealth signed them. So Anangu had Uluru for themselves – for about five minutes. Then they signed another paper giving a lease to the Commonwealth Government for ninety-nine years.

While all this was going on, there was an aeroplane flying over with a banner saying "Ayers Rock is for All Australians". It was a really nasty piece of work. We never found out who organised that.

After all the papers were signed, there was an opening *inma* by Tony Tjamiwa – dancing the *mala wapar* from Uluru. Then more *inma* went on nearly all night. I left for a while with my daughter Karina, and we had tea with the Governor-General and his wife. They had to go back to Melbourne, and I went to the *inma*. But by eight o'clock I just couldn't stay awake, so I sneaked off to my tent.

It was a really exciting day. And I can congratulate Bob Hawke and Clyde Holding, the Minister for Aboriginal Affairs at the time, for the part they played in handing back Uluru. They made Pitjantjatjara and Yankunytjatjara people very happy.

Since the handover, all my relations from Mutitjulu decided to make me the Chairperson of the Joint Board of Management for Uluru–Kata Tjuta National Park. And I've been there ever since. Aboriginal people have the majority on the Board, and others are from ANPWS and the Australian Conservation Foundation. Under the agreement the Northern Territory Government was to have one Labor and one Country-Liberal Party politician on the Board. There's a person from the Labor Party there, but because the Northern Territory Government was so upset with the handback, they wouldn't appoint anyone. It didn't bother anybody, and the Board was cut down to ten people. The Board of Management is going well: we are writing the second Plan of Management now. There've been some problems, but Anangu are learning to run a park, and ANPWS are learning to work with them. I'm happy to be involved in it.

* * *

In those first few years of AP and the Land Rights Act, it wasn't all mining and battling for land rights in places like Western

Australia and at Uluṟu. We did have some opportunity to do some things for ourselves – for our own development – instead of what a mining company or governments wanted. Ngaanyatjarra Council and AP started their own airline, and a buying service called Aṉangu Winkiku Stores took over supplying the community stores on the lands. Les Nayda did a lot of work helping us start up our own AP roads program. But the two things I'm most interested in and worked on is Aṉangu health and education.

I said before that when the Pitjantjatjara Council started in 1976, people talked about getting good education and good health care for themselves. In 1982, my good friend Elliott McAdam was at the Aboriginal Health Organisation in Adelaide, and he managed to get funding for a review of health on the AP lands. Trevor Cutter and John Tregenza travelled to all the communities talking to Aṉangu, and they wrote the Nganampa Health Report about the government Health Commission clinics on the lands and what should be done to make Aṉangu healthier. Pitjantjatjara Council set up an interim committee to implement the report. After meetings with the South Australian Government and DAA, they agreed to fund an Aṉangu-controlled health service in the AP area. We advertised for doctors and nurses and administrators and, on 1 December 1983, Nganampa Health was on the way.

One of the things Nganampa Health wanted to do besides giving people better health care was to find out just how healthy or sick Aṉangu were. Nobody really knew just how bad Aṉangu health was until then. I don't have all the figures, but I remember a lot of Aṉangu were going to the clinics as much as forty times a year, and they carried out ear tests on the kids and only seventeen had healthy ears. They found there were big problems, such as diabetes, high blood pressure, and kidney failure, and not many men lived to see fifty.

Glendle Schrader, my good friend and one of the people that started up Nganampa Health, thought that what we had to do was take a good look at why people were getting so sick. Glendle's idea was that we had to look at the health environment, not just the sickness people had. People's lives had changed: Aṉangu

179

don't just live out in the bush. They live on big communities a lot of the time and some of them live in houses. He came and talked to me about this vision he had. At first I didn't agree with him, but then I said I'd support what he wanted to do.

So Nganampa Health started up what they called UPK: looking at the showers and toilets and laundry in the houses, at the water on the communities, looking at what food people were eating, and looking at homelands. UPK workers found out that shower drains were blocked, water taps dripping all the time, toilets not working, rubbish all around where people were living. And they found out that a lot of the time Anangu were eating the wrong kind of food. No wonder they were getting sick. They came out with the *UPK Report* about all that and how to make the health environment better. And it's been very well received, not just by Anangu, but even people from overseas – like the Philippines.

Nganampa Health started educating people about what food to buy, like more fruit and vegies instead of eating white sugar and white bread and fatty meat all the time. And they'd tell Anangu living in houses that it's important to keep them clean. But communities have only one store – there's no K-Mart or supermarket like Woolies – and some store managers are very powerful. Sometimes they think it's their own store, and they can sell what they like. It's a bad situation, and it makes me angry. I've told community councils just to sack store managers who won't listen, but it's not that easy. I know there's whitefella rules that say you gotta warn them first or they'll sue you. But Nganampa Health has been trying to change things, and they talk to the community store managers and Anangu Winkiku Stores about getting healthy food to the communities, about getting mops and buckets and soap in the stores, even about getting pencils and paper and rubbers for the kids.

When the South Australian Health Commission was running the clinics, all of the decision-making was from Adelaide. Sisters lived on the communities, but doctors would just make a quick visit from Adelaide. Now, the health officers are Anangu, and Nganampa Health is making sure the bosses are learning what they need to know about running a health service. Nganampa Health offices are in Alice Springs, along with the Pitjantjatjara Council and other organisations for the Pitjantjatjara, Yankunytjatjara, and Ngaanyatjarra areas. The first health manager was John Pettit, then it was Glendle Schrader and then Kaisu. Their job has been to work beside the Anangu director, who is Robert Stevens right now, and to work in with the clinics on the lands.

One good thing about having our own doctors living on the communities is that babies can be born on the lands again. Anangu were always unhappy that the mothers would have to go away to the Alice Springs Hospital. And before, Anangu health workers really didn't do much. Since Nganampa Health started, health workers are getting good training, and they can do a lot of the jobs that the sisters used to do. And, now, when the doctors, sisters, and health officers work together, they use *ngangkari* – those people that know about traditional healing and medicine. A *ngangkari* woman or man might take a stone or stick out of someone's body and tell the patient, just to make sure, to go to the clinic and see the doctor or nurse. They work like that.

Nganampa Health still has problems, and the biggest one is the funding. The money they get from ATSIC and from the South Australian Health Commission is a help, but we need more money not just for clinics, but for other areas, community health, for example. We still miss out on a lot of things people have in the cities. And there are new problems. AIDS is one of them. Nganampa Health needs more money to educate people about AIDS – making videos and talking about it in different ways so Anangu will understand it's a serious disease. So far, I think they've done a good job because I don't think anybody is sick from that on the AP lands.

Another problem is getting good staff. We have been lucky with the professional people we've got, but they stay only about two years, and it's pretty hard to get good doctors and sisters to live away from the cities.

One spin-off from the work Nganampa Health has been doing – and this is for AP to work out – is land management.

181

Anangu are thinking more about leaving the larger communities and living out in small homelands. Small family groups can live healthier lives, mixing bush foods with what they buy in the stores, and they can look after the country. AP land management people are taking Anangu out so they can start looking after the country again. They're patch-burning it and going to the old rockholes and soakages, digging them out and showing the young people the places. And they're walking again, digging for rabbits, looking for tucker. People have been getting lazy having all those good whitefella things like motor cars and food from the store. They're doing the things UPK has been telling us so we can be healthier and live longer.

Number two is education, especially bilingual education. Schools on the lands are run by the Education Department in Adelaide. It's the biggest government department there, and they have the biggest budget: for schools, teachers, staff houses, and all the rest. Pitjantjatjara Council has been wanting to take on education since about 1988. The following year we started up the AP Education Committee and appointed Donald Fraser as the chairman. That Committee is to look into how AP could run education on the lands if we were given a chance – find out what sort of teaching and what would people learn. Right now, the school curriculum is put together down south in Whyalla. I'm not saying there's anything wrong with it, but it doesn't have much to do with Anangu and the AP lands. If we're going to run the schools ourselves, we'd have to rewrite it.

And that brings me to bilingual education. Our second language is supposed to be English, and I can see that knowing English is important. But I keep thinking: we've been with white people a long time and now they work for us on the AP lands, but every meeting, might be with a mining company or government, there's just one or two interpreters. People can talk their own language all right, but they can't express themselves in English. I can't understand that. I know Pitjantjatjara and Yankunytjatjara people can learn other languages. I think one of my grandfathers spoke nine different Aboriginal languages – maybe some were dialects. I know a lot of Anangu that can speak Arrernte or Warlpiri. But English – we haven't got a hold of it. I still have difficulties in pronunciation and lots of times my white friends help me.

Anangu kids have been going to whitefellas' school for a long time. Why is it no Pitjantjatjara or Yankunytjatjara person is in university or college? I'd ask my friend, Dr Cliff Goddard – he's a very clever linguist and he's worked with the schools: a lot of people come to Australia from overseas and they learn English here. All right, they might talk with an accent, but they learn it. We got bilingual education in the schools, so why don't more people know good English?

The Education Committee put out a report with the Education Department called *Two-Way Education* in 1991. In meetings, people said: "Look. Teachers can come here and teach our kids English. We'll teach them Pitjantjatjara and Yankunytjatjara. That's our job." That seemed right to me.

But then I'd listen to experts talking about language and I get confused. I remember, back in 1970, I heard about this language research in South America. They got two lots of kids: one lot was doing bilingual education, and the other was doing straight English. They found out that when kids learn only in English, they can read English all right, but those that learn bilingual, they can understand better what they are reading. So I thought then, well, this bilingual education is good. And later on my friend Dr Goddard would say if we don't have bilingual education Anangu might lose their language. So maybe that's right: maybe kids need to learn reading and writing in Pitjantjatjara and Yankunytjatjara first.

Then I think "But they don't have many books." I've heard of only one in Pitjantjatjara and Yankunytjatjara, telling you how to put windmills together or how to fix a motor car, that kind of thing. All the other books are in English. Then I look at Ngaanyatjarra people out west. When the United Aboriginal Mission had the school at Warburton, kids learned just straight English. And now those kids are grown up, and I hear those men and women at meetings using English really, really well. They still got their culture and their law. They still speak

Ngaanyatjarra, and it sounds beautiful to me, sort of musical. Not boring, like Yankunytjatjara. My kids are a bit like those Ngaanyatjarra people. Leroy, Rosemary and Karina have done very well on whitefella education, and they can talk and read and write Yankunytjatjara. I just stumble through, but they got a really good command of both languages. So why is it that Pitjantjatjara and Yankunytjatjara people can't be like that? Why are we stuck with just our own language?

When I look at bilingual education on the AP Lands, I think: "There must be something wrong here. What's it mean anyway, 'bilingual'? How long are kids supposed to do it?" What I see happening is a lot of schoolteachers, over the years, come here to teach English, and they finish up good students of Pitjantjatjara from the kids. They become expert in our languages, and some of them go down south and teach Pitjantjatjara in the colleges and primary schools. And our people are left behind, still talking Pitjantjatjara and Yankunytjatjara.

I started changing my ideas about bilingual education. I would talk to the teachers and my friends in education and I say maybe they should teach more English in the schools. But instead of helping, they think I'm having a go at them. They say, "Yami, you're just dead against bilingual education." But I'm not, I just want to find out what it is. I'm not very popular in that area. Still, I don't care, I don't want to be popular. Maybe I am a stirrer, a troublemaker. OK, I can live with that I guess.

I'm just worried about Anangu learning English because reading is so important. If they read and write and speak the English they can work in offices, they can go to college or university. They can learn to be accountants, mechanics, electricians, plumbers, builders. If we don't get a good education for them, we're always going to have the white advisers in the communities.

Now, I know other people rubbish white advisers for speaking for us, for deciding things for us. But in my opinion they've been good. White people that work for us are always thinking ahead, because they know what there is in the cities down south, and in Darwin and Alice Springs. In the cities they've already got community health, and we've only just started. And not just about health, but everyday things too, like water. Pitjantjatjara Council people find water for our communities and homelands and test it to see if it's drinkable. We don't know about those things yet. A lot of these programs need funding to get started, but we can't write the submissions because we don't have the education. So our advisers have to do it. And when they come back from the funding bodies with more questions, our advisers have to help us answer them. Then, if we get the funding, a lot of times a white person takes the job. Not because it's a white-fella job, but because we don't know how to do it. We don't have the education. It's no fault of the white people. We like them to have the jobs. There'll be someone wanting to know us then, someone who cares about us and wants to help us.

It's different with government people. They don't talk to us, they tell us what they think is good. The government has all the money and we depend on that. So sometimes we listen to them, but not very often. It's different with our advisers. They don't think for us, they put up ideas. It's up to us to think about them. So we talk about new ideas and we're learning. When the government people come up to tell us about what they want, like local government, we hire somebody who knows about that to give us advice. There's nothing unusual about that, about black people having advisers. Governments and mining companies have advisers all the time. When we got the adviser's report, we had a meeting about it and said: "You can keep your local government. We'll stay with Anangu Pitjantjatjara. That's our own body, our own local government."

So that's how it works with advisers, and we're happy to have them. But, in my opinion, if we don't educate our young people, train them, there's no future for us. Once I said to the community advisers and community council members that they should be talking with schoolteachers, finding out which young person is doing well at school. When there's a school holiday, they can take those kids and show them what the whitefellas are doing on the communities so they can get ideas when they leave school. I was saying that the community council should have

185

some sort of plan, maybe working through TAFE, to put those young people on work experience. They can work next to the bookkeeper, accountant, community adviser. I'd say I'm not against white people working on communities, they're good people, but they gotta train us. They can stay for maybe two years, and when they finish Anangu got to know that job.

But nobody really listens to me, nobody takes those ideas seriously. I suppose our own young people don't have the confidence to do those things. Maybe they don't want to be stuck in an office, they like to do what they like to do – be free. That might be right, but then we'll have non-Aboriginal people on the AP lands for a long time. I look at black people from other countries, I talk to them when they visit. It's tough for them, but they manage and they overcome their problems. They get the qualifications – the whitefellas' piece of paper – but they keep their own language, their own tribal beliefs and culture. Here, in Australia, it's suppose to be easy. We've got our land, but we haven't got the white people's piece of paper to say we're qualified. Those are the questions I ask all the time.

I hope this idea about "two-way education" will bring some changes. Maybe in a few years time, maybe ten years, we might see Pitjantjatjara or Yankunytjatjara people in college or university. I don't know. It's up to us, but everything we do depends on the government – we can't do without government funding. Our new health programs, homelands, and other ideas can't start without the funding. We can keeping working with what we got, but it's getting harder and harder to keep things going. I suppose that brings me back where I started, talking about mining and being independent. It's hard problems, and I think we've got to change.

Poisoned Land

I'm coming to the end now, but there's one last story I want to tell. It's the one that takes me back to my childhood, back to the days when I lived at Wallatina, and when I could see. A lot of people tried to forget what happened. I know I did, and my relatives too. And a lot of people tried to change what really happened. But this is how it started again for me.

Now, when was it? I wish I could remember what year it was. It was in Alice Springs, and I was at home with the flu. I was listening to the ABC program "A.M." on the radio, like I always do. They were interviewing this fella by the name of Sir Ernest Titterton. He was talking about the atomic weapons tests at Emu in 1953 and at Maralinga in 1956 and 1957. I was in bed, listening, but I didn't really pay much attention to what he was saying.

Then I heard the interviewer ask him: "And what about the Aboriginal people?" Sir Ernest Titterton says: "Oh, the black people were well looked after. We had two patrol officers in the area." He was talking like that. And I said to the radio: "Bullshit! I remember now! I was at Wallatina, and I remember that patrol officer used to come to the camp. All the Anangu called him *Kuṯa* – brother. Now which hand was it? He had three fingers on his right hand, if I remember rightly, and he used to shake hands with the left. That's right. His name was Mr McDougall."

Sir Ernest went on. Talking about the tests carried out at Emu, and then at Maralinga. Talking like everything worked out just fine. I was really stirred up by then. "Hey, this bloke is talking bullshit, he's talking the wrong way. He's only talking from his end, and he was all right. What about us? Oh, so they appointed two patrol officers to look after the blackfellas in the area? Well, I don't think we were all right."

All day I thought about what he said. And things started coming back to me, things I hadn't thought about for, I don't know, thirty years, I guess. I was a kid then and didn't really understand. Well, I still didn't understand, but what I remember wasn't anything like Sir Ernest Titterton's story. Somebody had to answer that person. A lot of people listened to him and they probably thought everything was all right when he said, "Don't worry about it, boys, we took care of the blackfellas." So what was I going to do?

I knew a journalist, Rob Ball, who worked for *The Advertiser* in Adelaide. I met him when I was at Mimili and he'd done a lot of newspaper articles for Pitjantjatjara Council and land rights. I was sure he would help me, so that evening I rang him at his office. He knew who I was, and we had a little bit of a friendly yarn, then I told him what I heard on the radio and told him I wanted to talk about the Emu bomb tests. Rob was pretty interested, because, he said, they were doing research on Maralinga. Most Australians didn't know anything about atomic tests in the 1950s, and the *Advertiser* wanted to bring it out in the open. So the ABC must've picked up what Rob Ball was writing in the newspaper and decided to interview Sir Ernest Titterton because he was the Australian boss for the tests then.

I told Rob Ball that when I was a kid I used to live with my family at a place called Wallatina. That was around the time they were testing the first bombs just south of Wallatina at Emu. I found out later it's about one hundred and eighty kilometres away. I said I remembered Mr McDougall, the patrol officer, coming to our camp and talking to the adults. I told Rob that one morning we felt the ground shake. Then I told him what happened next, about how we saw this thing coming over the camp and we'd never seen anything like it before. It looked like black smoke, but different – they called it a black mist in the newspapers later. When I said that, I could hear Rob turning away from the telephone and call out to somebody, "Hey, boys, we found the bomb!"

Rob talked to some other people too, ex-soldiers and this fella from the Atomic Veterans Association. They were trying to help those Maralinga soldiers who said they got sick because of the tests. After our story was in the paper, the ABC got Sir Ernest Titterton back and they asked him, "Well, whaddya think about what this Aboriginal man is saying in the newspaper about this black mist?" And he said, "Oh, it's just someone with a good imagination." That's all.

I saw Dr Trevor Cutter and some other friends after that, and talked to them about what happened at Wallatina. Things were coming back, and that's when I started thinking that maybe something happened to me at that time. There was a black mist or something like black smoke that came over us from the south, I am sure of that. I'll always remember it. And after the black mist came over us, everybody in the camp got sick. Then there was my uncle – the one I talked about before. I remembered him clearly as a healthy young fella before that day. One time my other uncle, Harry Wallatina, was on a beautiful horse, galloping flat out, and the one that passed away was running alongside. I reckon for a short distance he beat that horse. When he got sick, there were sores all over his body. They were open and they looked full of puss. The sun used to worry his eyes too, he couldn't look up, so he'd wear a cloth under his hat and hang it in front of his face. I used to sit down with him, help him warm up water in a billycan and give it to him, sitting alone in his *kanku*. Then I'd go away so he could wash himself and put this medicine on that he got from Mrs Cullinan. And I remember when he died.

I wasn't sure if other people had the same sickness, but I know almost everybody at Wallatina had something wrong with their eyes then. And they still do: one weak eye, or one blind eye, eyes off-colour. You can tell something's wrong. I'm not a medical man, and I don't have any records, so I can't prove anything, but it's true: all those Wallatina people have eye problems. It's very interesting, that's all. Anyway, so I started thinking that maybe the tests at Emu had something to do with me being blind. I didn't think there was anything wrong with my eyes before the black smoke came over us. But I know I could see with only one eye when we left Wallatina for Mimili.

The Advertiser came back to me again, I don't know how many months later. They asked me more questions and wrote another article. Around that time, Pitjantjatjara Council staff went out and started talking to Anangu on the lands about the black smoke or what they were calling radiation fallout. And people would say to them: "Oh, yeah. That's well known to us, but we never, never talk about it." The Anangu told them a bit about what happened then, about the black mist and about the sickness.

After the second newspaper story, Robert Stevens (the secretary of the Pitjantjatjara Council at the time) came to see me and said: "Don't talk to the newspapers. Just slow up. The Pitjantjatjara Council will help you. We'll talk to the Commonwealth Government." By that time the South Australian Government had come out openly, saying the tests had nothing to do with them: the Commonwealth Government had made a secret agreement with the British to carry out the tests.

I went to Phillip Toyne, our lawyer, and told him what Robert said. He agreed with him: "You can talk to the newspapers about general things, that's all right. But nothing else. Robert's right: the Pitjantjatjara Council might be able to help you." Which they did, and I was very glad about that.

In the first round the Pitjantjatjara Council came out publicly and asked Malcolm Fraser, the prime minister, for a royal commission into the tests. But he wouldn't agree. Then a representative from the Federal Government, Mr Hancock, came to Alice Springs for a meeting with the Pitjantjatjara Council executive. He said if we had anything more to say, we should write to the Government and they'd work something out. We thanked him for his help, but told him "No thanks." Later on, that same mob came out with a couple of reports about what I was saying. But instead of showing their human feelings and offering to help me find out about the black mist, they just crucified me. Looked like all they wanted to do was protect something.

Anyway, nothing much happened after our meeting in Alice Springs. Then, maybe four years later, one of the ex-soldiers from Maralinga started talking about a lot of things that went on during the tests. He was dying of cancer, so he wasn't worried about the Official Secrets Act. I think he said he seen Aboriginal bodies when he was there. The journalists from the newspapers and television never let up, just kept on pushing the Federal Government for answers. I thought they were really wonderful. And I really appreciate what that soldier said on our behalf.

While that was going on, the Pitjantjatjara Council organised a meeting with all those Anangu who knew about what had happened at Wallatina. It was the thirtieth anniversary of the first test at Emu, and they got together at the same place where people were camping when the black mist came over. Our advisers asked people questions and David Batty from CAAMA made a video of them talking about what they remembered.

We took that video to Canberra and showed people in the new Labor Government. Department of Aboriginal Affairs people at that meeting were understanding. They showed a lot of concern about what we were saying. Then we had a press conference, and the journalists saw the video too. We talked to politicians while we were there, and I remember the Australian Democrats and some of the Labor senators were very good, like John Scott from Adelaide, Michael Maitland, and then there was Clyde Holding from the Government. But other Labor people didn't support us at all. But the Government still didn't do anything.

By this time I was thinking more and more about the bomb, still trying to put the pieces together. I kept thinking about what men and women older than me had said on the video. I was only a kid then, so I didn't remember everything, but they were saying the same things: about the black mist and the sickness and death. And I was getting more and more convinced that the bomb had something to do with Wallatina people having something wrong with their eyes. With my eyes. I didn't know about any other health problems, but thinking back about people getting sick, and some dying, and what my relations were saying, it just looked like the atomic tests had something to do with all of it. We needed a royal commission to find out, that's what the Pitjantjatjara Council had been saying for four years now. Titterton and his crew and the Government were on the other side, saying everything was all right. But I knew everything wasn't all right. I do remember what happened to us. I do remember there was something unusual about that black mist or cloud or fallout or whatever it was. Titterton didn't know; he was on the other side of the fence. He wasn't going to listen to our story.

Pitjantjatjara Council decided to keep the pressure up. So they had the idea of sending me and my wife, Lucy, along with our lawyer, Richard Bradshaw, to London. We were going to talk to the British ourselves if the Australian Government wasn't going to do it. Shorty O'Neill, an Aboriginal man and a long-time fighter for Aboriginal rights, gave us some contacts from when he lived there. Richard talked to the British people in the newspapers, radio and television and told them we were coming. We got the money somehow, and off we went.

As soon as we got off the plane in London and went through customs, a bloke from one of the newspapers interviewed me in his car. After that, we worked flat out. I won't go into all the details, but we had a lot of meetings and got a lot of publicity. We met with the ex-soldiers that worked at the Monte Bello and Christmas Islands bomb tests. They were very sympathetic, but they said they couldn't tell us everything because of the Official Secrets Act. And they were still trying to get something from the Government themselves. The BBC World Service interviewed me. They said they were going to put what I said on the radio three times, and that about one hundred million people would hear it. We talked at public meetings and had a press conference at the House of Commons. One very important part was talking to those British scientific people. They were really courteous, letting me use my tape-recorder and listening to our questions, but they weren't giving anything away. Well, that's what they thought. Later on, back in Australia we transcribed the tape and gave it to the royal commission. The British lawyer reckoned that I tricked them.

After ten days, we came back to Australia. It was in the

Australian newspapers, about what we had done in Britain, and one radio station in Adelaide, 5DN, interviewed Richard. The South Australian Government started to get really vocal then, telling the Commonwealth Government they weren't happy about the Maralinga business. The Atomic Veterans Association kept pushing hard, calling on the Government to bring everything out in the open. Not long after, in July 1984, the Federal Government announced that they were going to have a royal commission. They appointed Jim McClelland (he is nicknamed Diamond Jim) as the commissioner along with two others, a man named Dr Jonas and a woman named Dr Finch.

Now that there was going to be a royal commission, it meant there was going to be a lot of work for the Pitjantjatjara Council. First they had to find two outside lawyers to act for Anangu, and they got Geoff Eames and Andrew Collett. Maureen Tehan, one of the Pitjantjatjara Council lawyers, worked with them, and so did Dr Heather Goodall, a historian living at Ernabella at that time. Geoff Farrow, seconded from DAA, was looking after the administration side, and Alexis Ormond, an Aboriginal woman, was going to co-ordinate all the information coming in. But Phillip Toyne wasn't going to be involved, and Richard Bradshaw had other things to do. I was very disappointed that Richard couldn't do it because he'd done a lot, interviewing me about what I remembered and helping to get the royal commission, along with Phillip, of course.

There were a lot of Aboriginal people involved, not only from our side, but from Maralinga and Western Australia. Our two anthropologists, Susan Woenne-Green and Daniel Vachon, had been working with Anangu, interviewing them about what they remembered and, along with Dr Cliff Goddard, they translated the Anangu stories for the lawyers. Dr Heather Goodall helped them as well. Our workers did the best they could to find out what happened, but there were lots of problems. We knew what we had seen, but they wanted information that we couldn't give them, and they wanted it because they knew white people would ask us questions and wouldn't believe us. It was a long time ago – the two bombs at Emu went off in 1953 – and we

193

didn't know times and dates when the black mist came over. We didn't have calendars or clocks then, and even if we did, we couldn't read them. And we didn't have medical records, because there was no clinic at Wallatina and no white doctors treated us. Our workers knew about other sicknesses that Aboriginal people had around the same time, measles or flu. We didn't know what we had then, and I was confused about measles coming at the same time, before or after the bombs. The only people that could tell us were Tommy Cullinan and Mrs Cullinan, and they had both passed away.

When Geoff Eames and Andrew Collett had all our papers ready, the royal commission came up, and I think they made history when they sat down with people at Wallatina. Auntie Merdie Lander, who had lived just north of Wallatina at Sailors Well, was a wonderful witness. Richard Bradshaw brought me down to Marla to give my evidence, but I lost him after that, along with Phillip Toyne and the other Pitjantjatjara Council workers. When it was over, I just didn't want to be involved any more. It was all very sad for me, and for my relations, remembering things that happened, talking in front of all those people about personal things that we just wanted to forget. I was sick of it.

I think it might've been about a year later, after the royal commission got evidence from Maralinga Aboriginal people, and had gone to Western Australia and overseas to England, they came out with their report. To me, they did a good job, and I want to congratulate Diamond Jim and his team for the effort they put into it, giving the British a hard time. There were two hundred and twenty-two recommendations, and seven of them had to do with us.

Sir Ernest Titterton's story about taking care of the blackfellas wasn't looking too good. The royal commission found that the first bomb they let off at Emu (Totem One they called it) shouldn't have been carried out that day. The weather wasn't right, and they should have known it was too dangerous. They said that a black mist or fallout from Totem One did come over our camp at Wallatina. It fell on our land, on me and on my family, and all the people living there. The bloody Australian and British Governments didn't take enough care of us. I don't think they really worried about it, and I'm still angry for what they did. I still say our people suffered because of it, only we didn't have the times and dates and medical records. So the royal commission made an open finding: they said they just didn't know one way or the other if Aboriginal people at Wallatina got sick and maybe died from the black mist. Maybe we'll always be in the dark about it. There's one thing though: white people in Australia knew a lot more about what happened on their own home ground. A lot of Japanese people were surprised when, in 1989, I visited Japan and told them that nine atomic bombs had been let off on mainland Australia in the 1950s.

The royal commission also made a recommendation for group compensation. We've been asking for that money to be put in a trust account, like the American Government did for the Bikini Island people. Some of that could go to Maralinga Tjarutja people for homelands, health and education in the Maralinga area. But, for some reason, the Federal Government hasn't agreed to a trust fund, so ATSIC has the money. We're still working on it. And our lawyers are still working hard to get individual compensation. Almost six years after the royal commission came out with their report, the Government hasn't decided on that yet.

The biggest problem is what to do with the radiation still in the ground. It looked like the Australian Government was left with the job, because the British reckoned they'd already cleaned everything up in 1967. It was going to cost millions and millions of dollars. The Government set up a committee of five scientists to look into it. I was disappointed that our lawyers weren't quick enough on that one. I still think that Pitjantjatjara Council and Maralinga Tjarutja should have their own representative on that. I understand there will be another committee to look at the report and we will be involved.

Part of looking at the radiation still there was to find out if Aboriginal people living on the land might still get sick from it. Maralinga Tjarutja got two anthropologists who had worked with them a lot before, Kingsley Palmer and Maggie Brady, and they found out how much sand people might eat from cooking kangaroos in the ground, where people went out for bush tucker, and things like that. What they found went into that report by those five scientists, and they've made their recommendations for the clean-up. They found out that the most radiation is at one of the test sites called Taranaki. Still, it was going to cost around $600,000,000 to do the job properly. Pitjantjatjara Council and Maralinga Tjarutja will need to get a consultant to advise them on the report. People at Maralinga are really worried about the radiation because there's a lot of it still in the ground, but they're just as worried about what will happen to the environment if they try to clean it up.

So, at the end of it, we were glad there was a royal commission. If it hadn't happened, the Australian and British Governments would have left it buried deep in the ground so nobody could have known. The story came out in the open and something is being done. But most Aboriginal people wish they never had the tests. We never did find out if we got sick because of it, but we know there is poison on our land and we might never get rid of it.

And I never did find out if one of those bombs made me blind.

EPILOGUE

My story's not really over, of course. I'm living at Wallatina again – that's where I wrote this book – and I'm still working for AP and the Pitjantjatjara Council and Anangu on the lands. I might even get to tell you about what happens next.

I still think about some of the things that happened to me, some happy and some sad, and I probably always will. I think the saddest one was when I was in the hospital in Adelaide, and the doctors were looking into my eye with the red torch. I couldn't see people's faces, I couldn't see anything at all except that red light. And I still remember it. It was the last thing I ever saw.

And I think about Lucy Lester, my wife, and the support she had given me since I met her in 1965. A lot of things happened to me since then, like getting the opportunity to leave the Institute for the Blind and go to Alice Springs. She helped me through all of it: welfare work in Alice Springs, station work at Mimili, the land rights movement I was part of, and all the rest of it. And all that time she raised our three beautiful children: Leroy, Rosemary and Karina. Rosemary's married now to a lovely young man, Harold Howard, and we have a grand daughter, Kiki, and a grandson, Robert James. I'm really fortunate in that way, and a lot of it is because of Lucy.

When I look back there are two people I'll never forget. One is the late Pastor L. J. Samuels and the other is the late Georgie Turner, my friend and interpreter. I think that's when things started happening for me, different things from when I could see. But it was also a sad time for me. I felt just helpless when they told me I was blind, and I knew that I would always have to depend on somebody.

There were a lot of special things too, like getting the Order of Australia for my work with Aboriginal people. But one I really remember just happened lately, when I got an invitation to go to Sydney and meet Nelson Mandela. For a long time I'd wanted to meet that man, hear his voice in person, to touch him. And it was tremendous. I had tears in my eyes when I shook his hand. He's been struggling in Africa with his people for a long time and even after twenty-seven years in jail he is still strong and alert. And when I listened to him, I could see that what's happening in Australia to Aboriginal people is the same as what is happening to black people in South Africa in a lot of ways.

I suppose there's a lot of other things too, but I don't want to go over it all again. Just one last one. It was 1967, and Lucy had gone to the maternity ward at Queen Victoria Hospital in Adelaide. It was a day I'll always remember. The hospital rang me up at work and told me – how do you say it? – I was the father of a bouncing baby boy. I could hardly believe it. I don't know how long I stood there, holding the telephone, but anyway I had to go back to the brooms. When I got inside the factory, all the fellas were singing out: "Well, come on, Jim. Tell us, what is it?"

I had that smile on my face I get sometimes, and sang out to my workmates: "It's a boy, everybody, a bouncing baby boy. Another boundary rider, just like me."

IAD continues the work begun by Yami Lester and Jim Downing: assisting community development for Aboriginal people and providing cross-cultural education between Aboriginal and non-Aboriginal society. IAD now offers its students a wide range of accredited courses, distance education facilities and a library/resource centre.

IAD Press produces a wide range of books and reports based on research and course-work being carried out at the Institute. The language list includes dictionaries, grammars and learner's guides in the main languages and dialects of Central Australia; the cross-cultural information list includes health and nutrition titles, land rights, oral history and autobiography.

Most IAD Press publications can be ordered through good bookshops, or direct from the Institute. If you would like to know more about IAD, or would like a copy of the IAD Press catalogue, call or write to the address below:

IAD Press
PO Box 2531
Alice Springs
NT 0871
Australia
Ph: (08) 8951 1334
Fax: (08) 8952 2527
Email: iadpress@ozemail.com.au